CONSCIOUS PARENTING

ALSO BY NICK POLIZZI AND PEDRAM SHOJAI, O.M.D.

Exhausted

Trauma

ALSO BY NICK POLIZZI

The Sacred Science

ALSO BY PEDRAM SHOJAI, O.M.D.

Focus

All of the above are available at your local bookstore,
or may be ordered by visiting:

Hay House USA: www.hayhouse.com®
Hay House Australia: www.hayhouse.com.au
Hay House UK: www.hayhouse.co.uk
Hay House India: www.hayhouse.co.in

CONSCIOUS PARENTING

A GUIDE TO RAISING RESILIENT, WHOLEHEARTED & EMPOWERED KIDS

PEDRAM SHOJAI, O.M.D.
& NICK POLIZZI

HAY HOUSE, INC.
Carlsbad, California • New York City
London • Sydney • New Delhi

Copyright © 2021 by Rising Tide Productions, LLC

Published in the United States by: Hay House, Inc.: www.hayhouse.com®
Published in Australia by: Hay House Australia Pty. Ltd.: www.hayhouse.com.au
Published in the United Kingdom by: Hay House UK, Ltd.: www.hayhouse.co.uk
Published in India by: Hay House Publishers India: www.hayhouse.co.in

Indexer: Joan Shapiro
Cover design: Michelle Polizzi • *Interior design:* Nick C. Welch

Cataloging-in-Publication Data on file at the Library of Congress

Hardcover ISBN: 978-1-4019-5904-3
E-book ISBN: 978-1-4019-5905-0
Audiobook ISBN: 978-1-4019-5955-5

10 9 8 7 6 5 4 3 2 1
1st edition, September 2021

Printed in the United States of America

For our children, and for kids everywhere.

CONTENTS

PREFACE

The COVID-19 pandemic changed the game for parents everywhere. Women dropped out of the workforce in record numbers to care for and raise their children. Millions of kids were without access to broadband and the internet, which made remote learning and connecting to friends and loved ones nearly impossible. Kids faced loneliness and isolation. And many families experienced food insecurity, job loss, and economic hardship. While many families, especially in the United States, have begun emerging from the pandemic, these challenges and others still exist, and we have yet to know the full impact this experience has had on our children.

We imagined this book long before the pandemic and economic crisis upended parents' lives everywhere. Seemingly overnight, parents were thrust into impossible positions with having to juggle working from home and remote schooling, while others were on the frontlines and risking their health and well-being, while still others were forced out of work. Parents and their children have gone through so much already, and we're not on the other side of this pandemic and economic crisis.

As parents too, both of us have struggled. We, and our wives, have agonized over planning healthy meals, limiting screen time, managing our kids' social isolation, assisting them with their homework and remote classes, and helping them cope with big feelings.

While this book was originally written for a nonpandemic life, we still found ourselves turning to many of the tips and strategies that you're about to read to help us raise our kids during this difficult time. Little did we know how universal these insights would be. At their core, the suggestions can help us navigate parenting more confidently, create deeper and stronger connections with our children, and bring greater awareness to our thoughts, emotions, and reactions as parents.

Being a parent is the greatest honor, privilege, and responsibility we have ever known. It also challenges us in ways that we never expected. No one asked to live through, let alone parent, during this historic moment. We recognize the extraordinary pressure you're under, and we honor your love and commitment to your children. Our wish is that you can use this book to inspire and guide you on your parenting journey. Our hope is that the suggestions you're about to read will help you through the most difficult and harrowing moments of parenting as you teach your children to become whole in their minds, bodies, hearts, and souls.

Stay present.
Pedram + Nick

INTRODUCTION

Being a parent is an incredible experience.

It's also terrifying.

The world looks nothing like what it did when we were kids growing up. Today, parents and children are confronted with a lot of unknown variables and experiences that we don't have good strategies for.

Parents have to find ways to raise resilient, wholehearted, and empowered kids while navigating numerous challenges like: increasingly advanced technology that has placed countless devices and screens into the hands of babes; a food supply that is grown using loads of toxins and chemicals that can disrupt our kids' health, behavior, and moods; a culture driven by hyperconsumerism that leaves our kids addicted to external sources of happiness, buying, and possessing material items; existential threats like climate change, natural disasters, and mass shootings that leave kids terrified, anxious, and depressed about the world they will inherit; an outdated education system that fixates on test scores and rote memorization, leaving kids with fewer opportunities to explore their imagination and curiosity, or to develop resiliency, independence, moral reasoning, and critical thinking; a Western culture that subscribes to the belief that for our kids to be "successful," parents must keep them busy, exposing them to everything—from music lessons to sports to clubs—instead of allowing kids to just be kids.

No wonder parents often feel overwhelmed, exhausted, and scared. It takes a lot of discernment, awareness, and the ability to make conscious choices to help guide our kids through these experiences.

The answers aren't always obvious or intuitive, yet we want them. We need them.

We have dedicated our careers to helping people heal. Nick has battled health conditions like blackout migraines that modern medicine couldn't cure and that led him to seek shamanic healing in Peru. As a documentary filmmaker, he has trekked through the jungles of Central and South America and the Caribbean islands searching for and documenting the alternative healing practices of shamans, medicine men and women, and healers.

Pedram has also wandered through Central and South America, as well as East Asia, on his way to becoming an ordained priest of the Yellow Dragon Monastery in China, an acclaimed qigong and kung fu master, a master herbalist, and a doctor of Oriental medicine.

As entrepreneurs, we've started, grown, and operated successful businesses, and each of us has written numerous books individually and together. Everything we do has the same intention: to help heal people and this planet.

As much as we're devoted to our shared mission, it's dwarfed by being dads. Nick and his wife are parents to two boys, while Pedram and his wife have a son and daughter. Raising emotionally intelligent, mentally resilient, physically healthy, and spiritually strong kids is *the most* important mission that we've been gifted.

It's also the hardest—it's fulfilling, but hard. We know we're not the only parents feeling this. Parents today live life at warp speed, trying to juggle all our responsibilities and commitments as bosses and employees, friends, brothers and sisters, sons and daughters, community members, and husbands and wives. We're trying to keep ourselves healthy and nurture our mind-body-heart-soul connection, while leading meaningful careers.

There's a lot of pressure on parents to be perfect, to get everything right, and to do it all. But no one can do it all, and in the pursuit of this unattainable goal, we often shift into autopilot. We start unconsciously parenting. We aren't fully present. We're distracted. We're responding and acting without thinking or reflecting first. We sweep things under the rug because we don't want to upset the balance or we don't have time to focus.

Often, we aren't aware of how we show up as parents. It's only later, when we feel like we're failing our kids, that we start thinking that something needs changing. We may notice, after the fact, when we snap or get impatient when our kids ask us questions. We notice after we keep saying no to going outside, playing a game, or reading a book with them. We notice when it's the fifth night in a row that everyone is eating a different dinner at a different time.

Both of us have lost track of the number of nights when we've lain awake in bed feeling like the worst parents in the world because it seems like we don't have enough time, energy, attention, or knowledge to get this parenting thing right. And that's a scary place to live. No parent wants to fail their children.

If you were nodding your head to all of that, then welcome. We know you. We see you. We are you. We often feel overwhelmed and burdened by wanting to do right by our kids, yet sometimes, not knowing how.

We were venting our frustrations to each other one night, when we realized that we had to stop complaining and bemoaning the state of the world and get busy finding solutions for parents, including us. So we did what we always do when we need answers.

We went to the experts.

WHAT YOU WILL FIND

With our trusted film crew in tow, we visited with more than 50 of the world's leading parenting consultants, therapists, pediatricians, and educators. Like our previous books—*Exhausted* and *Trauma—Conscious Parenting* features their insights and collected wisdom.

We've organized the book into nine chapters, each covering a significant experience in your child's life: conscious parenting philosophies, early childhood development, technology, existential threats, consumerism, education, toxins, nature, and time compression. We open each chapter with a short story that the experts shared with us. Some details have been changed and woven together to protect identities and condensed for the book, but each offers a window into a common, modern challenge that parents solved using practical, simple solutions.

Next, we spotlight *Modern Challenges*. We can't deploy solutions unless we know what we're up against. We follow with a few *Turning Points*. These are specific moments that can challenge our kids and us. Turning Points will help ignite your awareness before we offer a few specific *Conscious Parenting Suggestions*. These are practical, easy, and no- to low-cost actions you can use today. Finally, we close each chapter with a *Conscious Parenting Challenge* designed to help you incorporate one suggestion into your daily life.

You can read this book cover to cover, or you can jump in where you want. We've written this book so that you can quickly grab it, flip to an experience that you're struggling with, and identify a few suggestions to try out.

While we've filled this book with dozens of suggestions (the most that we've ever included in any of our books), you may find some more useful to you than others, depending on your circumstance. Our best advice: find one chapter, pick one turning point, and work on one suggestion. Keep track and note any changes. If that suggestion seems helpful, keep it. If not, try another.

Our experts called these tips "suggestions" because that's what they are. As much as parents may long for one-size-fits-all solutions, there's no such thing. Use the suggestions to inspire you, to give you different tools, and to open your mind and heart to seeing, thinking, and responding differently to the experiences your kids go through.

This book is also a great tool to use as conversation starters with your spouse, partner, or co-parent. We both are incredibly lucky to be married to our wives, who are phenomenal mothers, women, and true partners. A lot of the information in this book gave us openings to talk with them about how we wanted to not only raise our kids, but the kind of families we wanted to build and support.

While we specifically use the term *parents* in this book, we're speaking to any caregiver—an aunt or uncle, grandparent, or adult who plays a critical role in guiding a kid through their childhood.

Raising kids is a huge responsibility. It is often stressful, terror inducing, and riddled with unexpected twists and turns. It is also one of the most fun, exciting, and meaningful experiences that we've ever had. We hope this book helps you to slow down; let go of your fears, insecurities, and worries; and relax into being a parent. Odds are, you're already doing way better than you believe. Have fun, learn, and enjoy this ride.

May this book open your heart, clear your mind, and help you create deeper, richer connections with your children.

CHAPTER 1

CONSCIOUS PARENTING PHILOSOPHIES AND PRINCIPLES

Vani was determined to lean in and have it all—a career and family.

On the outside, it looked like she had attained the unattainable, but on the inside, she felt broken.

At 39 years old, Vani was a top attorney at her law firm and a multitasking supermom of three kids (ages 4, 8, and 11). Every morning, Vani woke up at 5 A.M. and ran six miles, just like she had done since her law school days.

Vani prided herself on her stamina and how she only needed four to five hours of sleep. But lately, she felt a bone-weary exhaustion. She had to drag herself from bed every morning. She was chugging extra cups of coffee, sometimes as late as 4 P.M. It was getting harder for her to concentrate at work; she was making mistakes and her brain felt foggy.

And what made her feel even worse was that she had no patience for her kids or her husband, Rajat, who she knew also felt the strain of working full-time as a communications director at a major foundation while trying to raise their family. She knew that no one meant to hit her buttons, but every day it happened, and she would snap at them. She hated herself for this.

When her kids asked her to play with them, read to them, or take them to the park, she'd say yes even though she was too tired to be present or enjoy it. Vani found that her mind wandered to all the things she needed to do—people to call, emails to follow up on—and she often only half listened to what her kids said. She hated herself for this too.

I am becoming my mother, Vani would think when she'd see the disappointed or hurt looks on her kids' faces. Vani's mother had worked long hours trying to support Vani and her brother. Vani's dad died when she was seven years old, and her mother worked two jobs, which left her with very little time or energy for her children. Vani had sworn she'd be different as a mom, but now she wasn't so sure.

She also felt a growing distance between her and Rajat. After the kids were asleep, Rajat would try to connect with his wife, wanting to get physically intimate, but that was the last thing she wanted to do, even though she felt like a horrible wife.

Deep down, Vani knew she needed a break, and that her life had become unsustainable, but she didn't see any alternatives. Rajat had said that he was worried about her and wanted her to slow down, but what was she going to do? She wasn't about to quit her job—she was on track to make partner and she liked her work. She wasn't about to dial back on being a mom either—she had three young kids who needed her.

Vani did what she had always done and what her mom had taught her: she kept going. That was until one morning, when she awoke at her usual 5 A.M. but physically couldn't get out of bed.

MODERN CHALLENGES

We live in an overstimulated world.

We have so much information coming at us 24/7, so many demands on our time and attention, and so many distractions that we get overwhelmed. That sense of being overwhelmed seeps into our parenting styles—and we don't even realize it.

As psychotherapist Greg Steckler explained to us, there are two ways of parenting. The first is called *instinctual parenting*, and that's what most people do. Instinctual parenting is divided into three forms: undoing, redoing, or living your unlived life through your children.[1]

Undoing happens when a parent dislikes how they grew up, so they try not to do what their parents did, preventing whatever pain they had experienced as kids from happening to theirs. "I get to undo what happened to me and create a different kind of family," is often the thought process that drives parents who use undoing with their children.

If a parent had a great childhood, then they may want to give their kids the same experience—that's *redoing.*

Finally, if a parent looks back on their childhood and believes they could have been more successful in some way—whether that's socially, academically, athletically, creatively—then they may try to drive their child to succeed where they didn't. A parent who lives *their unlived life* through the child's focuses more on what they (the parent) need than what is best for their kid.

People fall into instinctual parenting patterns unless they bring more consciousness to how they parent, and then they have to have enough emotional independence to look at their kids and see what they need, what their ambitions are, what they are capable of, and who they are as unique spirits, and begin supporting that growth.

This requires maturity and deep self-awareness on the part of the parent. It means the parent must become a *conscious parent*. This is not one more guilt-ridden road trip you are going to take. Being a conscious parent can, in the end, help remove some of the burdens and obstacles that we face trying to raise kids in our modern world.

Conscious parenting is not a set of to-dos, a checklist to mark off, or hundreds of rules. Think of conscious parenting as a philosophy and a way of showing up and raising our children. It's about becoming deeply aware in all situations and experiences so we respond mindfully, instead of impulsively, to our children. As the stewards of our children's lives, it's on us to nurture, develop, and help them grow into healthy adults who feel connected in their minds, bodies, hearts, and souls.

How do we become conscious parents? Well, that's the focus of this book. But first, we need to lay some foundational philosophies before we dig into specific experiences you and your kids will likely have together. Our hope is that these philosophies will trigger mini-awakenings within you, helping you to see yourself and your role as a parent differently.

Conscious parenting is not some lofty ideal or goal to reach *some* day; it's a way of life for you to embrace and continually work toward *now*. More than anything, conscious parenting takes your willingness to commit to waking up, becoming aware, and acting mindfully. That takes work and practice, but we know you can do it.

The simple act of committing to becoming a conscious parent will ripple through your life and your kids in positive ways. You are about to embark on a journey, filled with possibilities for new outcomes, a different relationship, and a healthier state of being.

Be excited for a new present and future that you're about to create with your kids—we sure are.

PARENT, TAKE CARE OF THYSELF

Our kids depend on us to take care of them, but who's taking care of us?

Our culture conditions us to sacrifice ourselves for our kids. We mistakenly believe that's parenting, but by giving up all our identity, health, and energy, we actually end up sick, exhausted, and with nothing left to give.

"Children cannot be well, if parents are not well," Laura Kalmes, professor of education at Illinois State University and a mother of three, told us.[2] "Conscious parenting requires us to understand that our well-being and that of our children's are intimately related. In my experience parenting, there have been times when I thought that through self-sacrifice and self-denial, I would be a better parent. But I wasn't a better parent because I wasn't a better person."[3]

We have to be the ones to take care of ourselves, and that includes addressing our needs, wants, desires, and health. We can't expect our spouses or partners to. They can help and hopefully will support us on that quest, and vice versa, but ultimately, we are the only ones who understand what we need to stay healthy and whole.

Put another way: we have to put on our oxygen masks first, otherwise we'll be no help to anyone, including our kids. This is true in our relationships too, especially with our spouses and partners.

This isn't a new concept. Intuitively, we know we have to take care of ourselves; it's just hard putting it into practice. Sometimes we don't know what we need. Other times, we feel guilty and selfish. And most often, we don't see how it's possible with the countless demands vying for our time and attention.

We know that making time for yourself is hard. You face unrelenting pressures that make it feel impossible. We want to be clear: taking care of yourself is not being selfish; it's being a good parent.

Healing and self-nurturing are two of the most selfless acts and two of the greatest gifts you can give to your children and everyone in your life. When you make yourself a priority, you will have more energy to share, your body will feel better, your mind will be sharper, and your heart will be clearer.

When you take care of yourself, you will show up as a better parent, spouse, or partner because you will be a better—healthier—person.

Fortunately, our kids help us see when we need to invest more in our healing and self-nurturing routines. As Dr. Stephen Cowan, a holistic developmental pediatrician, told us, "Your child is your teacher. They are little Dalai Lamas. You don't have to go to some fancy retreat. They are asking for you to grow, and they will show you how."[4]

Our kids are experts on us. From day one, they watch our every move, studying and learning about us. They get us down better than any therapist, Zen master, or teacher ever will. They know what ticks us off, gets us excited and happy, and what makes us sad and angry.

Then they start playing us like a cool toy.

They'll think, *Let me see what happens when I do this . . .*

"Don't touch that!" we yell in response.

Okay, Dad gets really excited when I try sticking my finger in this light socket, cool. Now, let me see what happens when I say this . . .

"I said, please stop talking while I'm on the phone!" we say, exasperated from repeating ourselves.

Okay, Mom gets really mad when I keep talking to her while she's holding that thing to her ear. Noted.

Dr. Cowan calls these *growth buttons*, which he says are opportunities for us to heal, so we can develop ourselves and grow.[5] The more we develop and grow, then the more centered, healthier, happier, and more content people and parents we become. It's a win-win for our kids, ourselves, and our families.

So you have to answer: Will you get a good night's sleep?

Will you take care of your body by fueling it with healthy and nourishing foods?

Will you exercise and move to stay strong, flexible, and agile?

Will you meditate and work to calm your nervous system?

Will you talk with your partner and spouse, making intimacy and connection important?

Will you give yourself permission to work with a therapist or healer to address underlying issues?

Will you give yourself time each week for self-nurturing activities, whatever those are?

Will you make your health and well-being a priority?

You deserve to be healthy, and your kids deserve to have a healthy parent too.

Conscious Parenting Suggestion: Take Care of You

It's time to take care of you, so what do you need most now? To tuck into bed a half hour earlier for better sleep or to read that book sitting on your nightstand? Do you need to meditate? Eat healthier? Move your body more? Talk to an old friend? Spend more time connecting with your spouse or partner? A session with your therapist?

There are so many ways to heal and self-nurture. What you pick doesn't matter as long as you choose something. Give yourself permission to add it into your life for one week. If you can, aim for something you can do for at least 30 minutes. If that's too much, no worries. Do what you can. What matters is taking the step and making the commitment to yourself.

Make sure to talk with your children, your partner, or the other caregiver in your child's life about what you're doing and why. Ask them for their support. Tell them you need to make your health a priority and that you want to be an even better parent.

HEAL YOUR CHILDHOOD

Conscious parenting requires us to be in a healthy relationship to our own childhoods and with parents too.

No one escapes childhood without some experience that needs releasing and healing, and that may include our relationship with our parents. No one gets to choose everything that happens in our lives, especially when we are kids. But we do get to choose how we integrate those experiences, our understanding of them, and how they shape who we are as parents today.

Ignoring whatever unresolved pain or trauma came from our childhoods or our parents doesn't make it go away. Often, whatever pain that we're storing seeps into our parenting without us realizing it. "If your needs weren't valued, seen, heard, or respected enough in childhood, then often when you're in this dynamic again, but you are the big one, then unconsciously you may end up demanding your child listen, see, hear, value, and respect you at the cost of your child being seen, heard, respected, or valued," explained Taylor Ross, a trauma-informed parenting and education consultant and mother.[6]

Trauma and pain can get passed on from generation to generation —often unknowingly. This is called *intergenerational trauma*. In our book, *Trauma: Healing Your Past to Find Freedom Now*, we spoke to many psychologists and other experts who talked about how trauma can get passed from parent to child over generations. For example, if your mother grew up neglected by her mother, then your mother may have gone on to neglect you in your childhood. If that neglect went unhealed, then it may interfere with your ability to raise your children, and you could potentially transfer neglect to them. Often, intergenerational trauma happens unconsciously and unintentionally.

Trauma has a wide definition too. It can range from what's called "Big T" trauma, which includes living through natural disasters, domestic violence, or abuse to "Little t" trauma, which includes experiencing divorce, neglect, chronic stress, or rejection. With trauma, it's not what happens to us, it's how we handle an experience. If we are unable to process and integrate a difficult experience, then it can become traumatic and impact how we show up as parents.

Intergenerational trauma will get passed through lineages until someone breaks the cycle. It takes a willingness to revisit the past and examine the relationships we have with our parents today. That takes courage and strength, but it's worth it.

When you free yourself from the pain and trauma caused by your childhood or that's connected to your parents, you free your children too. It may take some time and the help of a trusted ally like a therapist or healer, but it's worth the investment of your time and energy.

Just think, you have the power to heal yourself *and* your children, *and* your grandchildren, *and* your great-grandchildren, and onward for future generations. Isn't that worth it?

Conscious Parenting Suggestion: Heal Your Inner Child

You don't need your parents to heal your childhood—you can do it yourself. We always advocate for seeking trusted allies to help you on this path, especially if you're dealing with long-held traumas like sexual or physical abuse or severe neglect.

However, if you want to try something at home, then write a letter to your younger self. In this exercise, you will speak directly to your inner child. You can pick any age, but if there was an age that was particularly difficult or a time when you struggled with your parents, then go with that.

In your letter, tell your child-self how far you have come, who you have become, and what you're doing now. Tell your child-self that you're with them right now and how you ended up okay, strong, happy, resilient, and loving and are now a parent raising kids. Tell your child-self that they will be okay.

It may seem simple, yet this exercise can have profound impacts that can completely change your relationships with your childhood, your parents, and your child's childhood.

BE A GUIDE

Does the idea of your child failing freak you out? Does it make you feel uncomfortable, sad, or angry? Do you want to protect them from all pain or sadness, embarrassment or shame? Do you want to fix whatever situation has gone off the rails?

You're a parent, of course you do! Yet, often in our rush to fix everything for our kids, we inadvertently leave them defenseless to life.

Our kids will get bad grades. They won't make a sports team or get chosen for a starring role in the school play. They will make hurtful comments to their grandparents (or us). They will make messes. They will have accidents. They will screw up. This is a part of being human and experiencing life on Earth.

Our children don't need us to be their solutions; they need us to be their guides.

Our role is to show our children how to maneuver through life's inevitable ups and downs, especially how to deal with mistakes. We're consciously using the term *mistakes* instead of *failures* because our kids do not "lack success"; they make wrong decisions and take wrong actions.

Every mistake is an opportunity for our kids to learn about this game called life and how to play it. Mistakes teach our kids about resilience and fortitude, perseverance and commitment, kindness and empathy, and what to do differently next time.

Through their mistakes, our kids grow into compassionate, strong, wise, and resilient big people, but they need us to show them the way. They need us to talk about what went wrong and what they can try next time. They need us to show them how to move through this world.

As you continue on this conscious parenting journey, tuck this into your pocket. Reflect on how you can help guide your child through all their experiences, especially when they make mistakes.

Conscious Parenting Suggestion: Think Out Loud

Parents make mistakes.

There, we said what everyone is thinking but what most of us (ourselves included) hate admitting.

We lose our tempers and yell at our kids. We make comments we wish we could take back. We regret not putting our phones or tablets down earlier. We feel guilty about giving our kids another unhealthy dinner out of convenience. We hate ourselves for not spending enough quality time with them.

We are humans doing the best we can. We need to find grace and to forgive ourselves. We're also not alone—all the generations that came before us, and all that will come after us, will experience the same thing.

When we embrace our mistakes and shortcomings, we also teach our kids that it's okay for them to embrace theirs. That requires us to be vulnerable and authentic with our children. It's not always easy, but our kids deserve it, and so do we.

Jenny Carr, an inflammation expert and mother, shared a powerful technique with us that we can use to guide our kids through their mistakes by first guiding them through ours. Her technique is borrowed from an old practice she used as a middle-school teacher when she taught reading and comprehension.

Her technique is called *a read allowance*. Jenny would read out loud a passage to her students and would periodically stop, saying, "Oh, I have a question. Here's my question," or "Oh, I have a prediction. Here's my prediction."

By thinking out loud and sharing her thoughts with students, Jenny taught them how to think about the texts they were reading. Jenny uses the same technique with her kids when it comes to her mistakes.

She will admit to her kids when she's made a mistake, how she feels about it, and then what she wants to do differently next time. "I thought it would be difficult to admit my mistakes to my children, but I was wrong," Jenny told us.[7] "Admitting mistakes gives my children an opportunity to learn. Not only do I model what it is like to reflect and to be okay with making mistakes, I teach them compassion for themselves."[8]

We model to our kids the process they will go through with their mistakes too. Plus, you can reverse this with your kids. The next time they make a mistake, you can coach them through the self-reflection, asking: What went wrong? How does this make you feel? What were you thinking when it happened? What would you do differently next time?

They may ask you what you think, or you may offer input, but in this process, you're guiding them.

As a bonus: you're teaching your kids how to be critical thinkers and how to move on when a mistake happens, instead of getting caught in the whirlpool of beating up on themselves, negative thinking, and judgment.

The next time you make a mistake, try telling your kid about it. Share with them what happened, how it made you feel, and how you're going to respond next time, and see how they respond.

SEEK CONNECTION

We live in a disconnected world, which is ironic given all the tools we have to talk and see each other over long distances and at a moment's notice. Still, people feel disconnected from their spouses, partners, friends, and family, including their kids. People even feel disconnected from themselves.

Disconnection plagues our kids too, but we have the power to change that.

If you take away nothing else from our advice, please take away this: commit to spending more quality time connecting with your kids, strengthening your bonds, and building a strong relationship with them. If you can build it now—no matter their age—you will create a foundation that will make navigating challenges later in life much easier.

It is never too late or too early to start.

Look for opportunities every day where you can dial in to your kid and fully focus on them. Look for spaces where you can engage them in conversations, activities, or shared moments or where you can show them that you're present and that you care. There is no greater way to show your child that you love them than by tuning in to them and giving them your attention and time. It's magic.

If you're not someone who usually says, "I love you," then start. Look them in the eyes and tell them.

If we don't take these opportunities to connect with our kids, no matter how busy we are, then our relationships won't develop in the ways they need to. We're going to raise lonely kids, and we'll feel that too.

We want to acknowledge that for most of us, it's not that we don't want these relationships—it's that we're running on fumes, overscheduled and overcommitted, or we may not know how to create them.

Whatever your situation, please go easy on yourself. This is not about guilt-tripping yourself. It's about being conscious that building a strong relationship needs to be at the center of your parenting. Set that intention and you will seek opportunities. Trust yourself in connecting with your kids. You are already a step ahead—your kids are hungry for connection; they want to spend time with you.

We must show up. Make the effort, show our kids we care, open lines of communication, and remember to have fun too.

Conscious Parenting Suggestion: Let Your Child Lead

Once a week, for at least 30 minutes, give your kids the reins. Let them choose an activity that you'll do together.

Your "job" is to let go and have fun. If that's finger painting, have at it. If it's tossing a football, do it. If it's having a dance party or playing dress up, do that. You may not like these activities, but who cares? You get to spend time with your son or daughter. You get to watch them light up, laugh, and have fun with you.

Sharing activities strengthens bonds. It creates more feelings of safety and security for your kids, and you'll be surprised, you may find your stress levels come down. As parents, we carry a lot of added stress and strain. We're so focused on teaching and guiding our kids how to fit into society, cultural and familial norms and etiquette, and how to be themselves that we can forget how much fun spending time and being with our kids can be.

BECOMING CONSCIOUS

Vani's body felt heavy and numb, and it hurt to move her arms and legs. Scared, Vani shook Rajat awake. He told her to take some deep breaths, relax, and just rest. He told her he'd get the kids ready and then they'd call the doctor together.

Vani's integrative doctor said that Vani was exhausted from all the years running on so little sleep, managing a full-time career and motherhood, being a wife, the long-distance running, and all the caffeine.

The remedy for Vani's burnout was to give herself a chance to heal.

That meant putting her health and well-being first. Vani's doctor prescribed a multiprong approach. Vani would get hormone replacements to boost her energy reserves in the short term. She had to cut out caffeine (slowly) and improve her sleep by aiming for six to eight hours per night. Vani had to stop the long-distance running, which was too much for her body to handle.

Finally, Vani's doctor suggested that Vani discover and add more self-nurturing practices into her life too.

These were drastic changes for Vani, but she talked with Rajat, who fully supported her, and together they created a "plan." At first, many of the doctor's suggestions were hard for Vani to make— especially cutting back on the coffee. But she started slowly, cutting her afternoon coffee and drinking just two cups in the morning, finishing both before noon. She went to bed half an hour earlier and slept an hour later in the morning. She replaced the long-distance running with walking in the morning and at lunch, and with the occasional online yoga class.

And she started taking a bubble bath once a week—it was her self-nurturing gift—and her kids and Rajat would "help." The kids would pour the bubbles into the bath and get the water started as Rajat lit a candle and put on relaxing music. It became a way to support Mom, and it actually made Vani feel good.

It took a few months before Vani's energy slowly returned, but little by little, it did, and with it, Vani felt like she could be more present and engaged with her kids and wasn't as impatient with them or Rajat. At work, she felt more focused and could concentrate again too. She also felt like she had more energy to connect with her husband, and she realized that their relationship was getting lost in the shuffle between managing jobs, kids, and the household.

Vani's battle with exhaustion prompted her to talk with Rajat about what he needed and how they could create a "plan" for him so that he didn't burn out either.

Vani still has many demands on her time and attention, and she often feels tired. The difference is, she knows what signs to look for before she snaps or feels impatient with her kids. When they hit her buttons, she realizes she has to look within herself first to see if she's been taking care of her needs, and if she hasn't, then she needs to make more time for that.

Conscious Parenting Challenge

For one week, pick a healing or self-nurturing activity that you can add to your daily routine. This might be going to sleep earlier or setting your alarm later. Stopping work at a certain time or not checking emails after 7 P.M. It could be going for a walk, meditating, or reading a book or magazine for fun. Pick something that feels nurturing to your mind, body, and soul, and pay attention to how you feel that week.

CHAPTER 2

EARLY CHILDHOOD DEVELOPMENT

Jackie felt like a failure.

It began with conceiving. Jackie and her husband, Marc, had tried for over a year to have a child, to no avail. The couple needed a fertility specialist to help. Jackie's sister and some of her friends had told her not to worry, that a lot of women needed help getting pregnant. But Jackie felt like there was something wrong with her, and she worried it was a bad sign—that maybe she wasn't supposed to be a mom.

But then Jackie got pregnant.

Her pregnancy went mostly well. Jackie had planned to have a vaginal birth—it was how her mom and sister had given birth. Jackie went to a midwife, whom she loved and connected with, and together they put together her birth plan. But Jackie's baby had other plans. He was a breech baby, who never turned, and nothing Jackie or her midwife did could get the little guy to assume the correct, head-down position.

Jackie had to schedule a C-section. That devastated her. It felt like she was missing an important moment of connecting with her baby and experiencing giving birth naturally. Marc suggested they focus on meeting their son, and that how he came into this world didn't matter if he was healthy and safe. Jackie knew Marc was right, but she couldn't shake the disappointment.

The moment her son, Jacob, was laid on her chest was the most beautiful, happiest moment of Jackie's life. And she swore to Jacob that she'd be the best mom ever.

But when she took him home, it felt like she couldn't do anything right. Jacob cried most of the time when Jackie tried holding him, walking him, or rocking him. He cried when she put him in a stroller and tried taking him for walks. He hated rides in the car or being put in a swing.

What wounded Jackie the most, though, was that she struggled to produce enough milk and had to supplement it with formula. At first Jacob couldn't take the formula either, because it turned out he was allergic to cow's milk, so Jackie had to use a soy-based formula.

After three months in, Jackie was worn out. She hurt physically and emotionally. She didn't feel connected to her son—as far as she was concerned, he didn't like her!

"What mother can't connect or understand what her baby wants?" Jackie cried to Marc, who told her everything was going to be okay, and they'd figure it out together.

But Jackie wasn't sure she believed Marc.

MODERN CHALLENGES

Learning that you're going to have a baby causes an emotional flood. You feel excitement and joy, and totally unprepared and terrified. Whether you planned the pregnancy or it came as a surprise, whether it's your first or third child, women want to "get it right," and men want to support their partners "the right way" and go along for the ride.

Moms especially, we know you deeply care about making sure you eat the right diet, take the right vitamins, get the right exercises and the right amount of rest.

Parents want "the plan" that explains exactly what we must do, when, and how. Like most new parents-to-be, both of us had plans for supporting our wives through pregnancy, how the deliveries would go, and how we'd welcome our children into this world, bond with them, and build our families.

But we learned very quickly: nothing in the parenting realm goes according to our plans.

That goes for the many parenting theories and books that try to tell us this is *the right way* to conceive, the right prenatal care, and how to bond and raise your newborn and help them develop in those early childhood years.

From conception through delivery, from that first year through the early years, there is no best or only way. Before you freak out, there's still hope. While many parenting or birthing books feel like they are meant to scare the hell out of you, that's not what we're doing here. There are some general guidelines and suggestions that parents can use to help create the *right conditions* for conceiving, carrying, welcoming, and raising a child who is healthy, happy, and whole in their mind, body, heart, and soul during those early childhood development years.

The recommendations are meant to help give you some tips and tools to move through this period with greater ease, more connection, and deeper awareness. Take what you need. Leave the rest. If you use different techniques, more power to you. Whether it's in this chapter or any of the others, the most important takeaway is for you to find what works for you, your child, and your family.

That will probably take experimenting, and that's okay. Be willing to try new techniques, and you will find the best ones eventually.

We also shine the light on the mamas, a little more than the papas. This isn't to take away from any of the challenges facing dads—which are real and need managing too. But we cannot ignore how it is women who experience the unique physical, biological, and societal pressures and expectations around conceiving, carrying, giving birth, caring for their newborn, and raising a small child.

We know it can feel terrifying learning that you're going to be a parent, and when your child enters this world, it often feels like you can't get anything right. But you will get it right for your child and your family. So go boldly through these turning points with a healthy dose of grace and forgiveness for yourself and your spouse, partner, and support systems.

Most of all, enjoy this ride.

During those early years, you get to watch your child experience and see the world for the first time. They'll giggle at the silliest things and let rip-roaring belly laughs fill the room that will leave you in stitches. You will get to introduce this brave new world of strange people, places, and things to them and see their wide-eyed delight and awe.

If we can let go of our stresses and worries—even for a few minutes—our children will remind us how amazing and beautiful this world is, and we will feel the deep connection and bond that forms between us and our children.

Embrace curiosity too. You get to meet your child, to see their personality develop. You get to watch as their bodies grow stronger and more coordinated, as they gain language skills and learn how to communicate with you.

Yes, it's exhausting and tiring—we don't know any parents who get out of the early years without running on some fumes. And it's also such a fun time, if you can allow it to be. Let your kids inspire you. Laugh with them. Be amazed.

And experience all that life and your kids have to show you in their early years. It's pretty amazing.

CONSCIOUS CONCEPTION THROUGH PREGNANCY

Conception. The first, second, and third trimesters. Different milestones, yet all interconnected stops on the same journey to bring a child into this world. There is so much to unpack during these stages. We're going to highlight some of the best tips, especially for mamas, that our experts shared on how to set the stage for conceiving and carrying your child.

We also encourage you to find the right doctor, midwife, OB-GYN, and other health practitioners whom you feel comfortable and safe with, who can support and guide you through these important stages.

As you read through the stages, also think about how you can openly communicate your needs to your partner or spouse. This goes both ways. Having clear communication channels now will create a stronger connection between the two of you that will help serve you both and your child better when they arrive. And if you don't know what you need, then share that with your spouse or partner too, and hopefully, you can find a path forward together.

Conscious Conception

When we intentionally make space for and call a soul into our family, it's called *conscious conception*. Through conscious conception, we clean and clear our energy, making mindful decisions that support our health and wellness so that we, in turn, become clear and healthy vessels to receive this soul and bring it into this world.

With conscious conception, pregnancy begins months *before* a woman conceives. She's preparing her mind, body, and soul to bring a child into this world, and that means she may need to clean up her diet—eliminating alcohol and drugs, upping her fresh vegetables and fruit intake (opting for organic, if she can), eating lean meats (free-range, grass-fed, antibiotic-free if possible), and eliminating processed, packaged, and high-fat foods. The mom-to-be will also evaluate her water intake, ensuring she's properly hydrating, getting a good night's sleep, moving and exercising her body, and also reducing stress.

And if there's a partner in the picture, ideally, they will also level up their lifestyle and health regimen—it's not all on the woman giving birth. Both parents-to-be need to be as healthy as possible. According to Robin Ray Green, a licensed acupuncturist, pediatric acupuncture expert, and mother, "In traditional Chinese medicine, we look at conception from the perspective of your kidney essence, what we in the Western world call our genes. When the mother and father come together at the point of conception, they pass along their essence, or gene, to the child, which means parents want to be in the best shape possible for when they're about to conceive. They can pass along vitality, if they are healthy, or imbalances, if they are unhealthy."[1]

Before the couple even tries to get pregnant, they are laying the groundwork to welcome their child, and in a perfect world, it would happen when they're ready, willing, and want to get pregnant.

But we don't live in a perfect world. Often, even with conscious conception, couples need help from doctors and fertility specialists. This isn't a failure on the part of the parents—it's just life in our modern world. This is as true for men as it is for women. "We always look at the mom's diet or the health of her eggs, but the health of the dad and his sperm is important too," explained Dr. Christian Gonzalez, a naturopathic doctor, who has worked in fertility.[2]

If you have the ability to choose how and when you conceive, do it. Start from a place of choice when you consciously and intentionally can make decisions about your health, sleep, diet, and stress levels. When you do, you create a healthier space to conceive a child in.

It can also help the parents connect to the experience of pregnancy more positively. "When you start from a place of choice in the process, you are able to connect with the experience of pregnancy from start to birth," said Haley Kaijala, a midwife and mother of three.[3] "There is also less work that mothers have to do to take down walls and traumas that can come up during accidental pregnancies. There is nothing wrong with accidental babies. My first two were, and I love them dearly, but it was also more work to attach to motherhood and parenting as opposed to my third pregnancy, when I was able to choose and then be mindful about my choices going forward."[4]

Allow the idea of conscious conception to excite and intrigue you instead of stressing you out. There really is no right or wrong way to conceive. It happens accidentally all the time, and parents like Haley still bond with their babies, and babies still grow into happy, loving, well-adjusted adults.

But if it's available to you, consider conscious conception as a way to connect with the experience, intentionally inviting it in.

The First Trimester

Once a woman has conceived, that first trimester becomes laser-focused on survival and trying to have a viable pregnancy.

For many mamas, it can feel like survival for them too. Hormone loads often rock a woman's world in unexpected and unpredictable ways. For many women, morning sickness strikes them. Certain foods can make them nauseous, and it can be hard to keep anything—even water—down. Some women experience intense heartburn and crippling fatigue.

The best advice our experts shared: ditch judgment about what or how this trimester should go and just get through it.

When it comes to food, now isn't a time for judgment either. According to our experts, women need to eat what they can keep down and tolerate, and call it a victory—because it is. For those women with a lot of nausea or sickness, protein can help settle the stomach.

Combining protein with easy-to-digest, simple foods like white bread or plain crackers can help. Peanut butter on bread, scrambled eggs, yogurt, or anything mild that can help get protein into a woman's body can make a huge difference for her.

Some women may find that they need to drink water over ice— cold beverages may be tolerated more easily. Sometimes sipping lemonade can help too.

No two women will experience their first trimester the same, so this milestone is about listening to what your body needs. If your body needs more rest, then please rest. If you need to reduce workloads and expectations, then please do that. If you can eat only white bread and peanut butter, then do it.

If you do have intense cravings, mention those to your doctor. They could be a sign of a vitamin or mineral deficiency. We've heard that intense ice cravings can be a sign of low iron. Your doctor can run blood tests to find out if you're missing something and then will help you get the right nutrients to keep you and your baby healthy and happy.

And for all the spouses, partners, and extended support networks, make sure you're supporting the mama. Ask her what she needs. Be aware and pay attention to what she's saying or if she looks more tired than normal, and do what you can to help her through this period too.

The Second Trimester

Once a woman makes it through the first trimester, then they often get a grace period where their bodies settle into pregnancy and they begin focusing on what's in store. This trimester is about planning for what's coming, building energy reserves, and getting back on the nutritional horse.

Assuming that the morning sickness and nausea have passed, most women can return to their natural diets (healthy, balanced, whole foods), which often include prenatal vitamins and supplements that help support the baby's development and the mom's health.

This is also a time when the parents will work with their doctor and/or midwife to create a birth plan, and one for a potential postpartum.

Many women also hit this marker and feel like Superwoman. They have tons of energy, and it can feel amazing (for many women, not everyone) compared to the hormone roller coaster they were riding in the first trimester. If you feel more energetic, then take advantage of it. Move. Exercise. Rebuild energy reserves, muscle, and stamina. You will need it later.

Go for low-impact activities like walking, swimming, or yoga, which can help you feel better, sleep better, maintain a healthy weight gain, and prepare your body for giving birth.

The Third Trimester

When the third trimester hits, it may feel like going back to the first trimester for some women. Your body has changed so much by now—it feels heavier, more cumbersome to move around. It's usually harder to sleep.

Many women experience extreme fatigue. You need more rest and relaxation, but you may feel guilty about taking that time. There are a million and one things to do before the baby gets here, from preparing the house to getting organized at work for whatever upcoming leave will be taken to giving other children in the home attention and care and support.

Getting proper rest and minimizing stress are some of the best, healthiest actions you can take during this period. This prepares your body and mind for labor. It will also naturally balance your hormones, which will then help for birth, potential postpartum depression, and breastfeeding—all of which are hormone derived.

Here's another PSA to all the spouses, partners, and external support systems—help the mamas out. Run errands, cook meals, clean, help organize, and take some of the to-dos off her plate. If you're unsure what help is needed, ask or say that you're going to provide meals every Monday or some other task that will be helpful but won't require any additional labor from them.

We'll say it again: take naps during the third trimester. Rest up for what's ahead. Sleep as long and as much as you can, because those first few months after your baby has arrived . . . sleep? It's not going to happen.

The third trimester is also a great time to seek external supportive care practices like acupuncture and chiropractic. This will help balance your body. As for movement and exercise, do what you can that feels okay. Movement will feel restricted, so stretching, yoga, and other gentle exercises tend to work better.

There is very little—if anything—that is predictable or controllable about conceiving or carrying a child to term. During each stage, it helps to try to pay attention to how your body feels and what it needs—whether that's rest, exercise, certain foods or drinks, or lowering stress.

The most important takeaway: no judgment.

We know, that's easy to say and difficult to practice, but it's true. Every experience of welcoming a child into this world will look different for each woman. Try to focus on making your health and wellness a priority, including managing your diet, sleep, exercise, and stress. This goes for both parents, but especially the mamas.

Conscious Parenting Suggestion: Set Your Intention

Conscious parenting gives us the chance to dig deep to discover why we want to become parents, how we want to parent, and who we want to be as parents. Setting our parenting intentions can be one of the most powerful exercises we can do before our child arrives.

"How you do one thing is how you do everything," explained Margaret Nichols, a meditation and mindfulness teacher who also teaches at a motherhood center.[5] "When we approach having a child, we have the opportunity before conception to say, 'What kind of intention do I want to set around having a child? How do I want to be as a parent? What is my reasoning for wanting to be a parent?'"[6]

As Margaret said, we ask these questions and set our intentions as a way to create the conditions for the most beautiful experience of parenting we can have.

Sometimes we don't have the opportunity to consciously set the intention or to choose parenting before we conceive. That's okay. As Margaret shares, we can set our parenting intention at any time.

So grab a sheet of paper and write your intention. Keep it focused on the positive and in the present. For example:

- "I am grateful for the opportunity to be a parent, and I am a caring, accepting, loving guide to this child."

- "I am blessed to be this child's guide through this world, and I will respect, listen, teach them how to grow into a strong, loving, balanced, kind, compassionate person. I am willing to learn from them in our shared experience, and I will love them unconditionally, always."

You can also do this exercise with your spouse or partner, each of you writing then sharing your intentions and then writing a shared intention.

After you've finished, put your intentions somewhere safe and look at them periodically. During especially difficult times, you can pull them out to remind you why you are a parent to help hold you accountable to how you want to show up and to inspire you toward your vision for yourself.

NAVIGATING THROUGH POSTPARTUM

We're cutting to the chase: postpartum depression is real, and it goes undiagnosed far too often. It's also such a big umbrella. Maybe it's not full-on, but you can't get out of bed or feel like you can't connect with your baby, and there is a blueness, a sadness, that can't be defined other than: blah.

We want you to know, this is normal.

The experts we spoke to told us that just about every new mom suffers from the proverbial "baby blues" to varying degrees. Moms bring their little one home and bam! Moms become isolated. Not by choice, but by circumstance. Their bodies have been ripped and torn. Their hormones are all over the place. Their bodies feel foreign to themselves. They are making breastmilk to feed an insatiable appetite that needs feeding every few hours.

There are diapers to change, clothes to wash, and a baby to feed, hold, comfort, and bond with. It's a lot for new moms to shoulder—too much. "A woman is going to be in this dark cloud after giving birth, and they're going to be in this almost survival mode where they need to take care of themselves and their babies, but it hurts to do it," said Haley Kaijala, a midwife.[7] "They power and muscle through it, because women are incredibly strong and they can do things through the darkest situations, but they can't see outside their own bubble."[8]

While we cannot eliminate or cure postpartum depression, we can try to make it more manageable for moms. "There's an old phrase that says, 'it takes a village to raise a child,' but it's not about the kid," said Margaret Nichols.[9] "The child is fine. They will survive. They're the most resilient little things. It's about the moms."[10]

Moms need support systems. Focus on building these resources during the second or third trimesters so that when you need to reach out, you know who you can turn to—from friends and family to midwives, medical professionals, and doctors.

The best advice our experts had for moms: reach out and use the resources available to you.

Seek help. There is no shame in leaning on a moms' support group or talking to a therapist about what you're going through. By addressing your health on all levels, it will help you to become a more conscious human being, who in turn will be able to bond and care for your infant even better.

For all the spouses and partners, we know you're probably exhausted too. Welcoming your child into this world, bonding with them, running off limited sleep, and the stress from having a newborn in the home takes its toll on you too. We are not downplaying your experience or what you're going through. If you need outside support, you should seek that too.

As spouses, partners, friends, and family, we need to step up and be conscious and aware of what's happening to the new mother.

That may mean helping to find resources to support our wives or partners, or encouraging them to use the resources they had gathered before the baby arrived.

It can also mean that we shoulder more cooking, diaper duty, and cleaning. Just saying, "I'll watch the baby. You go rest," can make a huge difference.

Moms need sleep to allow their bodies to heal and recover after giving birth, to restore their energy reserves (which will be low), and to help produce breastmilk (if they are breastfeeding their baby).

Please be kind, be patient, and go easy on yourself. You have just been through an incredible experience and have brought a miracle into this world. You will be exhausted on so many levels. You deserve to be cared for and supported by your spouse or partner, and your family and friends.

Reach out. Lean on them. And take care of yourself.

Conscious Parenting Suggestion: Walk in the Grass

It's very easy to cocoon inside the house, but getting outside for a short walk can help you feel more connected to yourself, your baby, and the world again.

You'll want to avoid the hottest or coldest parts of the day, but otherwise step outside and breathe fresh air. If you can, take off your shoes and walk on the grass barefoot while pushing your baby in a stroller or holding them against your chest. Feel mother nature. This will ground you, and if you're holding your baby to your chest, it will ground them too. It should calm and soothe them, just as it calms and soothes you.

Walking barefoot in the grass or on the ground is a form of grounding, which helps balance hormones, reduce anxiety, and increase the maternal bond.

ATTACHMENT PARENTING OR NONATTACHMENT PARENTING?

Parents often feel pressured to find the right parenting style, just like people feel the need to find the right diet. For the last few decades, *attachment parenting* has received a lot of attention. It's the philosophy that a baby needs physical connection to their parents as much as possible. For example, at night parents would co-sleep with their infant. They'd seek maximum skin-to-skin touching. They would carry their baby as often as they could, offering constant contact from the parents to the infant. Attachment parenting also strongly advises against childcare for children under a year and a half.

Attachment parenting has some lofty goals and ideals, and for those parents who feel it fits, go for it, but for those parents who feel it doesn't fit into their lifestyles—for whatever reason—that's okay too.

"There is a tension between attachment and nonattachment parenting that comes from asking a lot from women who are in different situations," explained Dr. Laura Kalmes, professor of education.[11] "Women ought to have the right to respond to their baby's needs and in intimate ways, and not in ways that induce enormous amounts of stress, and under the expectation that they get back to work and back to their lives, and their pre-baby weight and all these absurd expectations we put on women, if we took attachment parenting seriously."[12]

As Laura explained, "I wore my babies for two years. I breastfed them for three years. I slept curled around them for years, and it offered a lot of ease, but I could do that because I had a partner who allowed me to do that and who worked and had health insurance and made that space available to me. And I still burnt out."[13]

What if it's not about adopting a parenting style, but rather learning to meet the ever-changing needs of our kiddos?

"Being a good parent isn't about choosing a style that has a label on it. It's about figuring out what works for your children," shared Katie Kimball, an online kids' cooking teacher and a real-food blogger who helps families, including her own, create healthy meals.[14] "I would wear my babies all the time. For me, it was a win-win because they were generally happier and less fussy. I had babies who didn't like to be set down, but some babies do."[15]

Instead of worrying about the kind of parenting style we adopt, it's more effective to look at the primary needs that our newborns have and find how to give our babies what they need in ways that fit our lifestyles and household situations.

As Dr. Sam Rader, a psychologist, told us, there are four infant developmental needs that parents need to provide:

Safety and security. Our babies need to feel that this world is a safe place for them, they are understood, and they belong. It means our babies get fed when they're hungry, changed when their diapers are full, and rocked or cuddled when they need soothing. When they feel safe, they feel connected to themselves, to us, to the world, and to others.[16]

Containment. Babies need to be held often, and on skin to skin as much as possible. This is especially true for the first few months of their lives. Babies don't know where they end and the world begins.[17]

Knowledge that it is okay, even when things don't feel okay. Infants need their parents to help them absorb their difficult feelings. For instance, when a baby cries, their mother or father will pick them up, hold them close to their bodies, and rub their back, either gently or with a firm touch—whatever the baby prefers. The parent may hum or sing a lullaby. Like magic, the baby will quiet down. That's because Mom or Dad stayed with the baby through that difficult emotion. The challenge is not to rescue the infant too quickly, while also not leaving her alone too long. This teaches the baby that even through difficult emotions, they are okay—and that feeling of "okayness" will go with them through life.[18]

A **"good breast" experience.** As Dr. Rader explained, psychologist Melanie Klein had a theory about the "good breast" and "bad breast" experience that a baby can have, literally and metaphorically. A "good breast" experience is when a baby is hungry, they get fed. The milk comes easily, it tastes warm and sweet, and when they are full, the breast is removed, and the baby feels happy and content. The "bad breast" experience is when the baby is hungry, but the breast isn't there, or the baby isn't hungry but the breast is given to them to suckle, or they're trying to feed but the milk won't come out or it tastes funny or sour. That's the literal feeding, but the experience is about more than the calories, timing, and temperature—it's also about the maternal warmth that gets passed from mother to child, real care, and vital love that gets exchanged.[19]

Being with the baby, gazing at them, looking into their eyes with love and affection, warmth, and intimacy are key. "When a mother is able to give her child the 'good milk' that includes that vital caring, then the baby experiences their hunger as a good part of them that draws care and food toward them, and they learn that good things will come toward them, fill them up, and they will feel good," said Dr. Rader.[20] "The child is left with the sense that they are good, that something about them is good because their hunger is good and draws good things toward them, and that's a lifelong identity."[21]

Quick reality check: don't feel bad if you want to zone out and check your phone when you're up in the middle of the night feeding your baby, or if you take some 10-minute breaks. It's okay—and maybe scrolling through your phone, texting, emailing makes you feel like an adult and not just an all-you-can-eat buffet for most hours of the day.

There are few experiences—if any—in life that are more humbling than being a parent. Speaking from our turns and twists on this ride, we feel like failures almost daily. But we've found the more we can relax into being dads and seeing our kids (at all ages) as puzzles to figure out, the more fun we have had. We're less judgmental and harsh on ourselves, and more forgiving about our mistakes.

Babies pick up on our energy. So when they cry and we freak out trying to figure out what they need, that only makes them cry harder. It's not easy, we know, but try to relax, stay centered, and you will meet your baby's needs. We know it.

Conscious Parenting Suggestion:
Aim for "Good Enough Infancy"

Throw away right or wrong and what all the other parents are doing. Instead, focus on what's right or wrong for your tiny kiddo. Some infants love being held a lot. Some want to be next to you with you lovingly staring and smiling at them. Some babies love to be carried upright and facing out so they can see the world, while others may prefer being pushed in a stroller.

Be an observer and become the expert on your child. When they cry, see what happens when you gently stroke their backs versus using a firmer touch. Every infant and toddler will have their own preferences.

Try to stay cool and calm. No stress or pressure (we know, that's much easier said than done), and aim for *Good Enough Infancy*, as described by Dr. Sam Rader. "With good enough infancy, a parent only needs to get it right 30 percent of the time. So one in every three tries works. A lot of the time we're caught up in our own stuff, we're distracted, or we don't understand what our infant's trying to communicate. And that's fine. As long as we get it right, 30 percent of the time, the kid is awesome."[22]

Focus less on how you want to respond to your kid's needs, and more on how *they want* you to respond to them.

HELPING TODDLERS NAVIGATE THEIR INTERNAL WORLDS

A big part of guiding our children through their toddler years is helping them navigate their inner worlds as they reckon with their sense of self and their understanding of their place in the world.

To help you help your kiddo make it through this stage, we're looking at two major turning points: teaching kids to be independent *and* dependent, and what to do with all their big emotions.

Independence and Dependence

When our children reach toddlerhood, it's time for them to learn how to negotiate between their little and big selves. They are no longer totally helpless babies, dependent solely on their parents or caregiver. They have this big self that is emerging for the first time. Our children develop some independence—physically toddling away from us as they begin wandering, exploring, and experiencing the world.

When kids feel their agency and power, they begin to know themselves as separate beings from us. They're developing and testing out their identities. This is healthy, natural, and we need to support it.

And there is still a little self—a baby self—that is inside our toddlers and that needs nurturing and support. Our toddlers need to know that it's still okay to be small and dependent, and to need Mom and Dad.

For this phase to go off as best as possible, parents need to help their toddlers hold both the big and small parts of themselves. We need to acknowledge and celebrate the ways that our kids are powerful and independent, *and* we need to reassure and help our kiddos feel safe. They need to know that Mom and Dad will be there to hold, love, feed, and protect them when they need it. As our kiddos start to try things in the world for the first time, they will look back at us wondering, *Are Mom and Dad still with me? Are we still connected? Are they still looking at me?*

As parents we need to be right there, connected with them, encouraging them, and celebrating their independence. No acting or looking disinterested or anxious or frightened; our kiddos will take that to mean that something is wrong with them, or it's bad or unsafe to be independent.

If we can hold both the big and little parts of our kids, nurturing both sides, then our toddlers will grow up knowing how to depend on themselves and others. Being independent and depending on help is healthy and balanced.

If, for whatever reason, our toddlers aren't allowed this healthy balance—say they have to take care of a younger sibling or are expected to be a little grown-up—then they can adopt what Dr. Sam Rader says is a *premature coping style*, which means they will think of their own needs as bad or unmeetable. "Toddlers grow into adults who think they need to be big, in control, achieving, and giving to everyone else, and that they get their needs met through meeting others' needs. These are the people who are always volunteering, giving, showing up, and cooking for everyone else. I work with them as adults to learn that it's okay for them to need me, for them to need others, and for them to receive care, not just give it."[23]

Handling Big Emotions

As they're going between their big and little selves, toddlers will have emotional experiences that surpass their ability to cope. Think about the times you've seen your toddler become overwhelmed, enraged by frustration, have enormous tantrums, or bite, hit, or throw things.

Just as we have to help them navigate their sense of independence and dependency, we have to teach them how to safely communicate what they're experiencing on the inside. It's our responsibility as their guides to start equipping them with increasingly complex and nonviolent ways of communicating.

When we react negatively, we teach our kids that their expressions are bad, and they can feel ashamed of self-expression. They will carry this shame forward, which can lead them to either suppress their emotions or have violent outbursts that make communicating and relating to others more difficult for them.

The earlier we teach our kids healthy, nonviolent ways to express themselves, the better they will become at emotional regulation and communication.

"When we see children inappropriately expressing themselves, it's our opportunity to first affirm their experience, to affirm their internal reality, and to give them the language about what you are seeing when a child has fallen to the floor and tantruming or a child who got angry and threw a toy," explained Laura Kalmes, professor of education at Illinois State University and a mother of three.[24]

Laura says this is an opportunity for us to get in close and affirm our children's experiences with language, which teaches them to express in words what they feel in their bodies. She suggests using phrases like "I notice" or "I see" or "It seems like," and as our children become more verbal, we can invite them to fill in those statements by giving them prompts like, "I'd like to understand what's happening for you. Can you help me understand why you're so angry?" or "I can see that you are really upset. Would you like to tell me why?"

These discussions are invitations for our children to claim their experience and retain their feelings rather than giving them the sense that their feelings are bad. It also teaches them to use language to share their experiences so other people can participate. In that way, they learn they're not alone, and they don't have to face overwhelming emotional experiences by themselves. They can share them with other people who love and care about them.

From here, we show our kids what behaviors are okay and which ones aren't. "It's okay to be angry; it's not okay to punch your brother." "It's okay that you're frustrated; it's not okay to throw your toys."

We're constantly drawing the line between affirming our children's inner worlds—what they're experiencing and that all of it is okay—and informing them that the way their anger gets expressed needs to change.

Admittedly, when our kids are toddlers, this can be hard. They're still gaining verbal communication and understanding. Do your best to affirm their emotions while giving them age-appropriate outlets to help them release their feelings.

Emotion is energy. Energy cannot be destroyed, just transformed. It needs an outlet, and that will differ based on our kids' personalities. Some kids like to work through their big feelings using deep breathing, while others need a physical release like running. Some kids may want to draw or bang on pots.

This may take some trial and error to find what works for your kid, but it's well worth the investment and time.

Conscious Parenting Suggestion: Find the Emotion in the Body

To help your child understand their emotions, we can teach them how to find and identify the emotions in their bodies. We can make this a game. Go out in nature, play ball, laugh—just do something where you are one on one with your kid. As you're playing, stop and tell them when you feel an emotion like happiness or excitement, where in your body you feel it, and how that sensation feels.

Then turn it around and ask your kiddo *what* they feel, *where* in their body they feel it, and *how* the sensation feels. You're teaching them to explore their feelings without judgment and in the moment.

Then the next time your child has an angry or frustrated outburst, you can ask them to tell you where in their body they feel angry. "Some parents let their child go and it leads to chaos, and that's overwhelming and traumatizing for the child because that feeling and expression of anger can be just too much," explained Dr. Julie Brown Yau, who specializes in developmental trauma.[25] "We want to stay connected with our child and see if we can get them to identify where in their body they feel angry, because that's where the experience is taking place."[26]

You can affirm their anger and then give them an alternative outlet to express that emotion. Maybe you take them outside to run around or to kick a ball. Maybe you get them to take deep breaths or to scribble on paper.

Be creative. Find what works best for your child. Do this, and you will teach them important emotional regulation skills that will stick with them throughout their lives.

BECOMING CONSCIOUS

Marc noticed that Jackie seemed to be getting more depressed and anxious by the day, so he suggested that she talk with a therapist about what she was feeling and going through. At first, Jackie didn't want to, but she also felt like she wasn't connecting with her baby, and she wanted to feel that deep maternal bond.

Marc pulled out the numbers for some therapists that they had included in a postpartum plan they created during the third trimester. He sat with Jackie as she made the call and appointment. It was the best thing they could have done. Jackie's therapist said she was suffering from postpartum depression and that she also needed to release the pain and trauma from the unplanned C-section. It took time, but Jackie began working through her difficult feelings around Jacob's birth, and as she did, she felt better.

But Jackie also needed more help during the day. Although the plan was for her to stay at home with Jacob while Marc worked full-time, Jackie could use more breaks from childcare during the day to run errands, pick up around the house, or just rest. Jackie decided to ask her mother (who lived close by) if she could spend a few hours at their home a couple times a week, to help out. Marc also took over doing the nightly feedings and check-ins, so Jackie could get more sleep and rest.

As Jackie worked through her emotions on the C-section and got more rest, she started feeling more connected to her body again. And as she felt better, she saw her son more clearly and she was more able to try different techniques with him.

For instance, she discovered Jacob liked soft, gentle instrumental music, and when she played it in the background, it seemed to calm and soothe him. He also seemed to like it when Jackie gently rubbed his tummy or back.

Jackie began taking him outdoors more. She'd grab a soft blanket, lay it on the grass, and then put Jacob on his back. Then she'd lie next to him, play with his hands, and stare into his eyes, smiling and sending all the love she had for him right into him. He just loved it! He would smile and giggle, and Jackie felt her heart soar. Soon she started lying next to him in the house, on the floor, or on the bed.

As Jackie started feeling better all around, she was also able to pay more attention to Marc's needs too. For the last two months, he had taken over nighttime duties, but now Jackie split nights with him so he could get more sleep too. They also made it a point to talk more about how each was feeling, what each of them needed, and how the other person might be able to help. This became a nightly routine that really strengthened their connection and bond.

By the time Jacob's first birthday rolled around, many of the struggles had been left behind, and Jackie and Marc had begun talking about when they wanted to start trying for a second child.

Conscious Parenting Challenge

Help your kiddo find the emotion in their body! Make a game out of this. Try to go outside, kick a ball, go for a walk, or play pretend. Randomly stop and tell them how you feel. Say, "I feel excited! My stomach feels tingly," or "I feel frustrated. My chest feels tight." You want to pair the emotion with the body sensation. That means you have to dial in to your body first and pay attention (who said parenting was just one-way learning?). After you've shared how you feel and where you feel it, ask your kiddo. Be patient. The first few times, they may not understand. But stick with it, and they will gradually tune in too.

CHAPTER 3

TECHNOLOGY

Jake and Tara needed answers.

All their 12-year-old son, Tyler, wanted to do was play his video games, and his parents didn't know if this was healthy—emotionally, mentally, and socially—for their son.

Jake and Tara had tried setting limits. At first, they had allowed Tyler to keep his devices—a laptop, cell phone, and handheld video game console—in his room. But he was spending too much alone time in his room, and he was waking up in the middle of the night to play his games. Jake and Tara quickly put an end to Tyler keeping and using his devices in his bedroom.

But they were struggling to get him interested in other activities. When Tyler was younger, he had tried soccer and basketball, but he hated them. He played the trumpet in the school band, but he didn't take to it.

Tyler also didn't have many kids to play with. He was an only child, and there weren't kids his age who lived in the neighborhood. The few friends Tyler had from school were into video games too. Often, Tyler and his friends would play multiplayer games online.

While Jake and Tara wanted to curb Tyler's gaming, it was also one of the few social outlets he had, and they were afraid to take that away from him. At the same time, they were worried that he wasn't getting enough face-to-face interaction and he was spending too much time cooped up indoors.

But for all their worries, Jake and Tara felt conflicted. Both worked full-time and didn't get home until between 5:30 and 6 P.M.

during the week. Tyler got home from school around 3 P.M. The rules were that he had to come home right away after the bus dropped him off, and he had to start his homework immediately. He was a good student (As and Bs), and he often finished his work before his parents got home.

If he wasn't gaming, then what was he supposed to do?

Jake and Tara spent countless nights talking about whether they should limit his gaming and push him to find other outlets. But would that also take away his friends? Were they projecting their own judgments on how Tyler should spend time? Were they worrying too much and for no reason, and so should they just let him be?

Or was it healthy in the long run because it was his means of socializing?

Neither knew the right course for their son.

MODERN CHALLENGES

We live in a digital world where technology has revolutionized how we travel, communicate, learn, work, and socialize.

For the two of us, we grew up on the cusp of this brave new, connected world. As kids of the '70s and '80s, we had television shows, movies, and video games that kept us entertained. As adults, technology has given us tremendous professional and personal opportunities too.

Both of us live out west and in the mountains, Pedram in Utah and Nick in Colorado, where we get to raise our families in safe and healthy environments, while simultaneously collaborating with incredible professionals all over the world. We are so grateful for the lives we lead, and we can't imagine them without all the tech.

As thankful as we feel today, we're also a bit overwhelmed by everything, especially when it comes to our kids and technology.

Childhood looks nothing like what it did for most parents. Kids as young as one, get handed devices. Toddlers play with tablets and cell phones and navigate video-streaming platforms.

Kids have access to the internet, social media sites that constantly change and evolve, and video games that they can play alone or with multiplayers—with everyone playing from the comfort of their homes. Schools have brought technology into the classroom. Kids as young as first grade are being given laptops to bring home, and by third grade, some kids get assigned their own email accounts. And although most of us feel guilty about it, we use these devices as babysitters to keep our kids occupied.

The bright world of technology and devices has captured and mesmerized our kids. On average, children ages 8–12 spend between 4–6 hours using screens, and teens up to 9 hours.[1]

This is an extraordinary amount of screen time, and the jury's still out on what the long-term effects on our kids' development—social, mental, emotional, and physical—will be. Talk about terrifying!

Sometimes we want to unplug all the tech and tell our kids no more. But that's not realistic. There's no escaping the digital, device-filled world. It's here to stay, and if anything, it's just going to grow. Instead of fearing technology, we need to teach our kids how to use it to enhance their lives.

Navigating the landmines in our technology-saturated universe is no easy feat, but it is possible. You can teach your children how to place limits and boundaries on it. You can teach them about healthy content versus unhealthy, how to use technology responsibly, and how to find a balance between having fun on their devices and developing real, deep personal connections with other people.

The truth is, technology is a tool that can make our lives better, but it is not life.

If we're not careful, it is very easy for our kids to get overloaded and overstimulated with all their gadgets and gizmos. It's on us, their parents, to help them figure out the right balance. We can do this. We have to.

Stay focused on the purpose of technology in your kids' life—and yours. Teach your kids healthy boundaries and respect for their devices. Show them how to create loving, empathetic bonds with other people.

And remain vigilant about the most important "device" in your child's life—you.

The parent-child bond is one of, if not the, most precious human connections we can form in this universe. You don't need any technology, a device, or an app.

All that's required is your time and attention.

KIDS, DEVICES, AND ADDICTION

First things first. Our devices were intentionally designed to hook us.

Whether it's a tablet, phone, video game, or app, the powers that be in the tech world use what is called *persuasive design*, meaning it takes us very little effort to use the technology. The easier it is for us to use, the more we'll use it.

A lot of thought also goes into making our devices physically pleasing to the eye. Apple products are probably best known for this, with their sleek and simple design. Notice the bright, vibrant colors and pop-up notifications that catch your eye.

Every detail has been carefully chosen to engage you, to capture your attention, and to keep it. These tech companies and app developers want you to stay glued to their products as long as possible for ad revenue, to collect more information about you as a consumer, or to ensure you remain a loyal customer.

How they hook us is through our brain chemistry. Every time we check our devices or scroll through or post on social media, and with every video we watch, game we play, or email or text we check, we're getting dopamine hits that shoot through our neural pathways and make us feel good, excited, and curious. These are the same dopamine receptors that get activated when we eat good food, make money, and have sex.

Our brains become addicted to these dopamine hits, so we have to keep checking, keep scrolling, keep pounding refresh, and keep posting to feel good.

Now add kids into this mix. Kids, who have very little impulse control, whose brains are still developing, who live for instant gratification. It's not difficult to see how quickly they can become addicted to the stimulation coming from these devices. A recent report by Common Sense Media found that 50 percent of teens reported feeling addicted to their devices.[2]

"There is significant and growing evidence that social media and digital addiction is fueling the epidemic of teenage anxiety," explained Dr. Elisa Song, a holistic pediatrician and pediatric functional medicine expert and mother of two.[3] "Our kids, in their youth, are crying out that there's something going on, and rather than saying no to all technology, we need to understand what's going on."[4]

Knowing that our devices were designed for us to become addicted to them is a powerful first step toward creating better balance through making intentional choices.

Conscious Parenting Suggestion: Create Balance with Devices

No expert who we spoke to suggested removing all devices from our children's lives. That's unrealistic. But they all recommended being very intentional with how and when those devices were used and the way in which the use was supervised.

One-to-One Screen Time and Real-Life Play

Simply saying no to screens won't work. It'll leave our kids frustrated, and they'll find a way to get them, whether at a neighbor's house or from one of their friends. This leads to lying and hiding, which no one wants.

Richard Louv, a journalist and author of the bestseller *Last Child in the Woods: Saving Our Children from Nature-Deficit Disorder*, recommends a one-to-one ratio.[5] For every minute spent on a device, your child needs to spend a minute outdoors or playing with toys that don't light up and aren't plugged in. That could be wooden blocks, arts and crafts, dress-up and make-believe, kicking or throwing a ball—whatever is age appropriate.

"Kids find a way to solve their own problems," explained Richard.[6] "There are only so many hours in the day, so a kid is not going to be able to play a video game for four hours and find another four hours to play something else. One of our goals is self-awareness, so a child can learn to self-regulate, and that's what they learn with this method. They play a video game for thirty minutes and then they want to play with Daddy or roll around race cars that don't light up, on the floor."[7]

Try this for a week and see what happens. Do this with your child, letting them decide what kind of play they will do. It means you will need to be disciplined in holding them to their time limits, but if you can, you may find your child will develop healthier boundaries around using their devices.

Make Age-Appropriate Device Decisions

It's hard to know how much time to allow our kids to spend on their devices. The following guidelines offer some general advice that the experts we spoke to shared. These are not hard rules that you must follow, but rather suggested best practices that you can adjust as best suits your children.

- **Age 2 and under.** No screen time. "Kids are curious at that age," said Reena B. Patel, a child and educational psychologist who specializes in behavior.[8] "I believe in manipulative and engaging interaction, so letting them develop through touch and feel, and going through their other senses to explore their environment, is important."

- **Early preschool to kindergarten.** Now is when we should consider exposing kids to educational programs, whether that's on television, games, or apps. However, we should limit screen time on all devices to *no more than an hour.* That includes television, phone, and computer. We should make sure that we're present with our kids as they're watching or using these devices. Ask them questions like, What are you looking at? This helps to ensure they're absorbing the information and not just passively taking it in.

- **Elementary school through high school.** A lot of the experts agreed that device time should be limited to *no more than two hours per day,* whether that's for your 8-year-old or your 16-year-old. But there's a caveat. As our kids get older, it's more about what they're using the technology for.

"Screen time is not all the same," explained Alyson Schafer, an Adlerian family counselor and one of Canada's leading parenting experts and therapists.[9] "I'm looking at things like, are kids being active or passive? Are they entertaining or creating? It would be really hard to have a teenager and say, 'You can only be online for one hour' when they're going online to transfer money from a bank account, or they're playing a card game with grandma virtually, or they're checking their homework for tomorrow or the temperature to find out what to wear to school."[10]

As Alyson suggested, we want to look for balance and to nurture the proper use of technology. If our kids are playing a mindless game on their phones for three hours, then that isn't adding benefit to their lives. Alyson says we can help our kids be mindful about what they're doing online by teaching them how to identify the purpose the device serves. So is it for entertainment or recreation? Is it educational? Is it productive or creative? Is it functional by helping with daily life? Then we can talk to them about how they manage their time so that it's more balanced daily, weekly, monthly, and yearly.

CONSUMING MEDIA AND ENTERTAINMENT

Powerful storytelling helps teach our kids about what it means to be human, how to relate to other people, how to overcome obstacles and setbacks, and what it means to go on authentic emotional journeys.

Today our children have an extraordinary abundance of content to choose from. From movies to television to video games to videos, they can consume anything. There's just one question: Is the media and entertainment our kids consume enhancing their lives and contributing to their well-being, or is it an escape or distraction that is unhealthy?

So much of entertainment today is centered on fast-paced, aggressive adrenaline rushes that push our kids' fear, insecurity, and stress buttons, causing real biochemical reactions in their bodies. "We have five times more fear receptors than joy receptors in the brain, and the fear receptors get stimulated more quickly," explained Katie Kimball, an online kids' cooking teacher and a real-food blogger.[11] "When we're seeing that motion and when we're seeing the twenty-four-hour news cycle and social media with the comparison-itis game, our fear receptors are constantly stimulated, and it is addicting like a drug."[12]

When our nervous systems get stimulated, we shift into fight-or-flight mode and send cortisol and adrenaline pumping through our veins.

For our ancestors, all of those chemicals coursing through their bodies would have them fighting or running for their lives. But we are not often in physical danger. Instead, we're left sitting on the edge of our seats, stimulated, but without any outlet for all the energy running through us.

That's a very frustrating experience for the body.

It needs to move to release the energy and stimulation. For some kids, all that pent-up energy creates intense mood swings, irritability, behavioral issues, and attitude problems. Some kids also become more agitated, have trouble sleeping, or lose social skills. Some even struggle to slow down. They're constantly wired because they've fed their minds and bodies hours of this intense, high-octane content.

But it's not just the physical body we have to worry about; it's also our emotional and mental selves. The more violent, aggressive, and mean-spirited content that our kids consume, the more desensitized they become. It's not that our kids will turn to crime sprees, necessarily, but they can stop *feeling* to a lesser degree.

Feeling and emotion make us human by allowing us to empathize with others. Emotions allow us to understand ourselves too, and what we need to feel whole and healthy. When we're desensitized, we can't feel pain or love, anger or peace—we're just numb. We don't want our kids to be numb. We want them to be fully engaged, loving, and connected little people who evolve into fully engaged, loving, and connected big people.

Sometimes, when our kids consume violent or aggressive content, they don't always have the language to communicate to us what they're witnessing and how it may make them feel. They may not understand what they're watching, but they'll know something isn't right, even if they don't know exactly what. If they don't talk to us about what they're watching, and most kids won't unless we prompt them, then our kids will likely sit with those images, which can turn traumatic.

We're not saying that everything our kids should watch or the video and computer games that they play have to be positive and rose-colored. But as parents, we need to pay attention to what images and experiences get fed to our kids. We need to know whether they're only getting massive adrenaline rushes and becoming emotionally numb or upset, or if they're also taking in content that has real depth and quality that uplifts and inspires them.

It's easy for parents to use media and games as babysitters. Let's get real: everyone has at some point. This isn't to make anyone feel bad. It's about being aware and informed. It's important for us to know what our kids consume so we can help them understand what they're watching or playing. When we're tuned in to what our kids consume, then it's easier for us to make sure they take in more healthy content than unhealthy content.

This can start today.

This is on us as parents. Will some stuff slip through? Of course. It's like junk food. No matter how hard we try to give them clean and healthy whole foods, snacks and sweets sneak in. This will happen with their media and games.

But if we can make more effort to sit and watch what our kids watch, ask them questions about why they enjoy a game or show, talk to them about what's healthy versus unhealthy, and set boundaries around what they consume, how much, and for how long, all our seemingly small actions will go a long way to ensuring our kids consume media and entertainment that enhances their lives.

Conscious Parenting Suggestion:
Engage with the Content with Your Children

No matter their age, we should know the content our kids consume. This means we need to engage with them.

Watch and Talk about the Content with Your Kids
Sitting down next to your kids and being present (no scrolling on your phone) while watching a show or playing the video game can

make a huge difference in managing what is absorbed. It means engaging with your kids on the content too, asking questions about what they like or dislike. It means sharing what you think about it and how it makes you feel. It's asking your kids what they would have done if they were faced with the same challenge or situation.

This also allows you to be present to answer questions or to read body language. For instance, if your child stiffens up, widens their eyes, or looks frightened, you can say, "That's enough of this right now. Let's go play with the blocks."

This is conscious parenting—being engaged and aware of the experience you're sharing and adjusting in real time as your child needs.

Explain Unhealthy Content and Limits

To understand what's healthy versus unhealthy for our kids, we need awareness about what *we*, as parents, consume. The next time you binge a show or play a video game, try to pay attention to how you feel when you're consuming it. Think about why you like it, how it enhances your life, and how it could be unhealthy, or why it's healthy and how it uplifts you.

Once you have some answers about your own habits, then you can have more conversations with your kids about why you choose the shows you do.

Trina Wyatt, an entrepreneur and filmmaker, explained to us that when her daughter was in high school, all her friends watched the hit show *Game of Thrones*. Trina didn't want to watch the show. It was too violent for her, but coming from the philosophy "everything in moderation and don't make anything taboo, otherwise our kids will blow it out of proportion," Trina talked to her daughter about why she believed the show was damaging for *everyone*, whether they were a teenager or an adult.

"I told her, 'It's okay that everyone at school loves it. I can't watch it. I don't think it's healthy for you to watch, but you're getting to an age where you can make your own decisions. I'm not going to police what comes up on your iPad 24/7, and I don't want you to be influenced by what everybody in high school is watching. So let's have a conversation about what is healthy and isn't.'"[13]

When we talk to our kids about the choices we make, we are teaching them to make similar decisions themselves. It also helps them begin to connect the dots with how they feel while watching a show. Then together, you and your child can talk about the show.

The more language you use around healthy and unhealthy content, the more kids will understand why you may place limits on what they can watch, just like you help direct their eating habits too.

Help Kids Transition

If your kids are having a hard time stopping watching a show or playing a video game, try to find a solution together. Maybe you can set a timer and give them a 15-minute warning, then a 10-minute warning, then a 5-minute warning, and then a minute warning on when to stop.

"You want to enable and empower your child to control their own tech use," explained Teodora Pavkovic, a psychologist and life coach focused on parenting in the age of technology with an emphasis on character strengths and emotional intelligence.[14]

Teaching our kids how to quit and shift from a game or video to something else is one of the most important lessons we can teach them. Some kids struggle when their game, or any device, gets taken away. They may scream or have an aggressive reaction or outburst that can frighten us. If we remember the addictive nature of these devices and games, then our kids' reactions become more understandable. If an addictive source is involved, we will likely see overblown reactions.

The remedy is to give kids a transition from one activity to the next. Tell them, "You can play that game for five more minutes, and then it's time to . . ."

But if you know that your kid has a difficult time stopping playing games or transitioning from one activity to the next, try setting ground rules before they play the game. Set time limits so they understand the expectations. Explain that the game is designed to keep them hooked on it for long stretches of time, and if you were to allow them to play the game as long as they wanted, they'd probably spend 12 hours playing, which isn't healthy or safe for them.

If they really act up, explain that they'll lose the privilege to use the device the next time. And hold firm. Don't allow them to use it. Then bring it back into the rotation, and explain to them the time limit and the plan. If they act up and refuse to stop playing, then the result is they lose the chance the next time. Keep doing this, and eventually your child should learn to curb their behavior (which, really, is self-regulating their emotions).

CONNECTING AND LEARNING EMOTIONAL INTELLIGENCE

Our devices connect us to each other. Technology has removed time and space boundaries to allow people on opposite sides of the world to see and hear each other in real time. It's mind-blowing what we can do today.

Still, talking and interacting and engaging with someone through digital channels is nothing like being physically present with them. There is an energy that we get and give when we're face-to-face with other people.

When we're with someone physically, our neurological, biological, and chemical mechanisms kick into gear. We're paying attention to that person on so many levels that we're hardly aware it's happening. We're watching gestures, body language, and posture. We're noticing the tone of voice and facial expressions. We have about 42 facial muscles that do a lot of hard work to allow us to send messages to other people about what we're thinking and feeling.

Anytime we're in a room with someone, our nervous system is also turned on. Often, we're not aware of it, but our nervous system and brain are working to figure out if someone is safe for us to be around or if they're going to hurt us. We're filtering and processing unconscious information that we're picking up on from the other person.

Technology interferes with this deep, unconscious communication, and when it comes to our kids, too much device time puts our kids at risk for underdeveloping these important abilities. Many of the experts we spoke to mentioned how many children struggle with basic interpersonal, face-to-face skills. "Children are not able to maintain or establish eye contact in person, and that's important for their healthy development," explained Teodora Pavkovic, a psychotherapist and a parenting coach.[15]

The inability to make eye contact leads to other challenges too. "A child cannot develop empathy unless they're looking at another person because our ability to empathize comes from looking and identifying what's happening to someone," Teodora told us.[16]

Your child will use technology, but it's not a substitute for the real in-person experiences they get when they're with their parents, siblings, friends, and extended family. As parents, we need to remember that human contact, face-to-face interaction, and looking our kids in the eyes are just as important as teaching them how to read or add and subtract.

Also, kids often think they are more mature than they actually are. Their physical age does not match well with what they're being bombarded with on these devices. Everything from decision-making on what to share, who to share it with, what is safe content or material from a credible source, and so much else. If kids are left unattended with their devices, they can quickly go down slippery slopes.

We can't expect devices and technology to teach our children appropriate, responsible, and safe interactions with people. We have to do that. We have to help our kids develop the emotional maturity to use technology as a tool for connecting and learning.

Conscious Parenting Suggestion: Ante Up the Face-to-Face Time

Helping our kids develop emotionally starts with putting limits on their device time and being conscious with the kind of personal engagement we expose them to.

Bring Back an Old-Fashioned Game Night
Living in our digital age, it's easy to assume that old-school board games are a relic of the past. Except, that's not true. The market for board games keeps growing. Between 2017 and 2023, it is forecasted to grow by 9 percent.[17]

Why the demand? Because it's one of the few things parents can use to get their kids to sit at the table or on the floor, without electronics, and talk and play together.

Connecting over a game is one of the best bonding activities that you can do with your child. It gives them a chance to interact with you, to observe facial expressions, and to have fun.

This doesn't have to be stressful or hard. Pick one night a week, and make it game night. Make it fun. Keep your phones on silent, stash them in another room, turn off any movies or television shows in the background, and play. Put on some easy background music if you need to, pop popcorn, make some hot tea or cocoa, and have fun.

Stop, Look, Ask

In Teodora Pavkovic's practice, she has parents ask their children a series of questions. "It may seem a little awkward or weird, but I will have parents stop what they're doing, turn to their children, and ask them, 'What does my expression tell you? Does it look like I'm happy? Do I look like I'm amused and excited? Does it look like I'm serious? Does it look like I'm upset or sad? What are you getting from my face?'" Teodora shared.[18]

As Teodora explained, "Especially with the role that technology plays, we need to make sure that we do this with our children, especially when they are little, because they have a hard time telling the difference between different emotions inside themselves."[19]

The next time you're talking or engaging with your kids, take a time out and ask them what your facial expression tells them. They may need a little jump start, so give them examples. Make a face and tell them what you're feeling. This doesn't have to be hard. Make it a fun game to teach your child emotional intelligence.

Look Kids in the Eye

It is the easiest practice we can do. It's simple. It costs us nothing. And it will pay dividends for your child.

Make eye contact with them when you're talking and engaging with them.

It sounds so easy, but how often are you looking away at your phone, on your computer, or doing a chore while your child is asking you something? We all do it. As parents, we are professional multitaskers, but that takes away from our kids, especially when they're young.

As Teodora told us, "We say that the 'eyes are the window to a person's soul.' It is true, and it is important that parents make sure they look their children in the eyes as much as possible when talking to them. Not enough parents are aware of this."[20]

When we make eye contact with our kids, we're teaching them to pick up on all of those signals that another person sends. So the next time your kid asks a question, or you need to talk with them, look them in the eye.

THE SCREEN TIME DILEMMA FOR PARENTS

We tend to focus on the impact that technology has on our kids.

That makes sense. Kids are still developing—physiologically, emotionally, physically, and mentally—and they're so sensitive to outside stimulation that we need to look at how many hours they spend on their devices and consider the effects.

But we've forgotten to look the other way: *at parents*.

What are *we* doing with our technology? How much time are *we* spending on it? According to a recent Common Sense Media report, "On average, parents spend more than nine hours on their screens, with 82 percent of that time (almost eight hours) devoted to personal screen media activities such as watching TV, social networking, and video gaming, with the rest used for work."[21]

That's an incredible amount of time that we spend hooked to our devices. While we're tapping away on our phones and computers or scrolling endlessly through social media feeds, or checking emails and banging out responses at all hours, our kids sit there by themselves, get on their phones or tablets, watch television or fiddle around on some device—if Mom and Dad are doing it, why can't they?

"It's incredibly important to look at parents and this element of distraction, this element of absence, that happens when they're on their technology," explained Teodora Pavkovic.[22] "When parents are not physically and emotionally present in a moment—if they are texting somebody or emailing, checking maps, looking at the weather, or whatever it is—that impacts the child. With small children, especially, the most important thing for parents to do is to connect with them, to really be with them, to be present, to make eye contact, to have a lot of physical contact, a lot of that verbal back and forth."[23] Teodora said that when she's working with parents, she stresses to them, "With young kids, the only device or app that children need, is their parent."[24] Kids develop properly when they have deep connections with their parent.

As conscious parents, we want to be honest about our technology habits. This isn't to judge yourself, making you feel guilty or like you're a terrible parent. We get it. Parents are pulled in 1,000 directions, and we bet you're exhausted. It's not that you don't want to give this time and attention to your kids; it's that you don't know how. How do you put down your devices and walk away from them?

We'll admit, it's hard. We're as vulnerable as our kids to the technology addiction, and many of us have careers that demand our attention and quick responses.

Even so, we still have to find healthier ways to balance our tech use with our parenting. We need to get real and understand if we're overusing our devices and the quality of interaction with them. Are we addicted? Do we have to keep punching the refresh button and mindlessly scrolling social media feeds? Are we binging show after show, night after night? Are we behaving in ways that don't square with our values as parents?

These are the questions we have to ask and answer so we gain the knowledge we need to make adjustments in order to show up as the parents we want, and know, we can be. It's making adjustments so we can connect with our kids and give them the nurturing and love and guidance they need to grow.

We have to lead by example. If we don't create the conscious effort and model how to responsibly use our technology by putting it aside and being a human being—not just a human doing—then our kids won't learn how either. We would miss out on creating the deep human relationships with our kids that really are the best part of life.

Conscious Parenting Suggestion: Find Ways to Connect

Disconnecting from our devices and dialing in takes effort. Parents juggle multiple responsibilities and lead busy lives. That's why we need to intentionally make time to drop the devices and focus on our kiddos.

Create "Parenting Time"

Many of our experts suggested creating windows throughout the day solely devoted to parenting. That could be from 6–8 P.M. Devices get turned off, and you're focused on being present with your kids. During this time, you're eating dinner as a family, and the kids are doing paper-based homework or they're reading for school under your supervision. It's a time when you're having meaningful conversations and connecting.

If your kids are younger, then this could be bath time, playtime, or reading a story with them before they go to bed. You can also make mornings for "parenting time."

Whatever you're "doing," you're connecting and being fully present and focused on your children without distraction.

Have an Unplugged Box

With your family, you can create a wooden or cardboard box where all the gadgets get tossed into for a digital break. Maybe as soon as everyone comes home or before a meal, they toss their devices into this box and the lid gets closed for family time. You can start small. Try this for 30 minutes a day and see what happens.

Create Device-Free Zones

We can get intentional with connecting by creating places that are off-limits to devices. That could be at the dinner table or during meals. It could be when you're playing in the backyard or at the park. The car can be another device-free zone, and that includes when friends are in the back seat. There will be no texting or being on your phones or tablets. Instead, you're side by side communicating. The rules may be different in friends' cars, but at least you can establish your car as a place where meaningful conversations can happen.

Eat Dinner Together

It's shocking what happens when our families eat together at the table without looking at devices or being distracted. Conversations start. Eye contact happens. Facial expressions are seen. Sharing a meal as a family is one of the most powerful ways to connect and bond with your children at all ages. As kids get older and extra-curriculars or sports or school or friends and boyfriends/girlfriends start taking up more time, getting everyone around a table for dinner every night may seem impossible. Still, try to set aside at least two nights for everyone to eat together.

Dinnertime is sacred time in both of our homes. We check all our devices at the door and focus on being with our kids and wives and spending time together as a family.

It may be uncomfortable, especially if you never grew up in a home where this happened or if you're busy (which, we know, who isn't these days?). You may feel you don't have the time for this, but trust us: you can't afford to miss out and neither can your children.

BECOMING CONSCIOUS

Jake and Tara contacted a psychologist and parenting coach who specialized in working with kids and technology.

The first step was to track how much time Tyler spent playing video games. For one week, Tyler spent about 3–4 hours, often after he finished his homework and before and after dinner. The weekends varied depending on what Jake and Tara had planned.

The psychologist suggested that Jake and Tara switch their perspective from video games as being bad or good to more about helping Tyler to find more balance in his life. The psychologist also explained that if Jake and Tara wanted Tyler to find other interests and hobbies, the two of them would have to get more involved in helping their son to find what those were. They couldn't expect Tyler to discover them alone.

After much discussion, Jake and Tara decided on a multipronged approach. First, they wanted to meet Tyler where he was. If he loved video games, then they wanted to understand what he was playing and why he enjoyed them. Because he was going online to play multiplayer games, it was also important that they do an online security and safety refresher.

One night, after dinner, Jake asked to sit and watch as Tyler played with his friends. Tyler had given him that look that said, "Seriously?" Wanting to keep it light, Jake laughed and told Tyler to make a joke. "Just tell your friends, 'My dad's here. It's lame, I know, but he wants to see what we're up to.'"

That night, Jake sat and watched and asked a lot of questions the psychologist had recommended, including how Tyler knew the difference between talking to strangers and talking to friends and what kind of information he shared about himself. And it turned out that Jake had so much fun watching that he asked Tyler to teach him how to play and suggested they play together sometime.

Next, Jake and Tara wanted to reduce the amount of time Tyler spent gaming every day. One night at dinner, Jake and Tara told Tyler that they were going to make some adjustments in the house. They stressed Tyler had done nothing wrong, nor was this a punishment. They knew how much he loved playing video games and they wanted him to keep enjoying them. They also wanted him to have more balance with how he used his time.

That evening, the three of them came up with a new schedule. First, Tyler would become responsible for walking their dog as soon as he got home from school. Tara was nervous about this, but the psychologist suggested that giving Tyler little bits of responsibility here and there would help him. It did. Tyler took to that responsibility very well and it gave him a sense of independence, while also making sure he spent time away from the technology.

Next, Tyler was allowed to play video games for an hour a day, as long as the dog had been walked and his homework was finished.

Once Tyler's parents got home, the video games would be turned off. Tyler would also be responsible for helping his parents make dinner and setting the table. Jake and Tara also decided to establish a weekly, weekday family board-game night, and on Friday or Saturday, Jake would watch and/or play a video game with Tyler.

On top of this, Jake and Tara committed to arranging more face-to-face time with Tyler and his friends. And they also talked to Tyler about trying different after-school programs or area camps. Tara explained that he didn't have to know if he would love it—he would only know that after he tried it.

Together, Tara and Tyler researched different options in the area, and Tyler said he wanted to try an outdoor, wilderness survival camp for middle schoolers.

All of these adjustments took some time, and they needed tweaking on occasion. Tyler still pushed to play his games for more than an hour, and Tara and Jake had to hold steady. But overall, an hour a day seemed to work well. With all the other activities he was doing, Tyler was building a more balanced life and a healthier relationship to his electronics. He was spending more time outdoors and in person with people, and he was trying new activities.

More than anything, Jake and Tara felt relieved that Tyler's video games seemed to be more a part of his life, rather than all of it.

Conscious Parenting Challenge

Make dinnertime, family time! For one week, we want you to eat dinner as a family, leaving all devices in another room and turning off all screens. We'll allow music—it sets the mood. Focus on appreciating the food, the time, and being with your kids. Ask them about their days, what new thing they learned at school, who they played with, how they're feeling, what they're looking forward to. Tell them about your day. Look them in the eye. Smile at them. Talk and be present and bond and connect.

CHAPTER 4

EXISTENTIAL THREATS

Malcolm didn't know what else to say.

He was driving his seven-year-old son, Sam, to day care, and Sam kept asking him about tornadoes. This wasn't the first time. For over a month, Sam had repeated the same question: "What happens if a tornado hits our house?"

Every time, Malcolm would tell his son, "It's not going to happen. We live in New England, and we don't get them here."

"But what if we do?" Sam would usually reply, to which Malcolm would say, "There is no reason to be afraid. Stop worrying."

Except Sam didn't stop. Whenever it started raining or a thunderstorm rolled in (it was midsummer), Sam's body would shake and he'd ask his father if the storm meant a tornado was coming. Frustrated, Malcom would typically say something like, "No, Sam. It's just a regular storm. No tornadoes. You are *fine*. I am fine. Everything is fine. Trust me. Please, stop worrying."

Malcolm was trying to stay patient, but he was getting frustrated. It seemed like Sam wasn't listening. Malcolm didn't understand where Sam's fears were coming from, and he didn't know how to ease his son's anxieties.

MODERN CHALLENGES

The world feels scary, because it is scary.

Every day, we're bombarded with horrifying images, stories, and for many of us, everyday experiences that threaten our existence. From mass shootings and natural disasters, to wars and diseases, to racism and police brutality, to climate change and environmental collapse, we are living through events that challenge our capacity to cope, survive, and feel hopeful about the future.

If you want to shield your kids, to protect them from the violence and mayhem, the despair and fear, that's a normal response.

Trying to raise kids in our world today is frightening. We want to acknowledge that. Every parent we know—including ourselves—has moments where we feel horrified imagining the future for our children.

If you have moments where you're anxious or depressed, it's okay. You're recognizing the duality in life, but we also can't let the darkness overcome us. We have to find a way through it, because our kids are counting on us. They need us to get it together and show them a way forward, because not only do kids take their cues from us, but many feel terrified and gripped by an existential dread that the world is ending and their futures are bleak.

Rather than remaining paralyzed thinking "it's so much harder today than before" or "the future is so hopeless," what if we reframed our existential fears to say: maybe now is just *different*?

We're not trying to minimize what's happening today; the world does face enormous challenges that threaten our sense of security and survival. And, throughout recorded history, it seems the story of being human is the story of facing existential crisis and having to overcome the threats.

Human history is littered with atrocities and bleakness, and it's also filled with incredible stories of resiliency, perseverance, and people coming together to solve problems and work toward a better future.

The antidote to our children's existential suffering rests with hope.

If we have hope for the future, so will our kids. That doesn't mean we deny the reality and difficulties we face. It means that we show our children that even in the darkness, we can find light. Our children's ability to face the world as it is today and to still feel and sense hope begins with us and how we see the world. It begins with the seemingly small acts that we choose every day, and that our kids see us taking. It begins with our openness and willingness to talk with our kids about the scary stuff and helping them to process their feelings while we share ours too. No matter how chaotic the world around our kids becomes, they can learn the tools that will help them remain strong, kind, grounded, and resourceful. We can teach our children how to understand and process their emotions in healthy ways, while showing them how to take action even when they feel scared or uncertain. We have the power to imbue our children with an inner strength and that sense of hope that will guide them through their lives.

So take a deep breath. Round your shoulders up, back, and down. Hold your head up, and walk bravely through this world and its existential threats.

THE EMOTIONS OF PARENTS

How do *you* deal with your existential fears? Do you stop and consider your emotions, or do you push them aside and try to ignore the uncomfortable feelings?

"If we're anxious and worried, and we're talking about a threat in an anxious and worried way, then our kids won't listen to our words," explained Alyson Schafer, an Adlerian family counselor and one of Canada's leading parenting experts and therapists. "They can see from our faces, and from how we're carrying ourselves, and they'll interpret our signals as, 'Boy, if the adults in my world are scared about this, I should be scared too.'"

We want to aim for *calm confidence*. In this emotional state, it signals to our kids, "Yes, I'm concerned about this threat. If no one was concerned about climate change, then things would only get worse. And here's what we are going to do individually and as a family to do our part in helping to find solutions."

Calm confidence acknowledges the threats as real and shows our kids how we deal with our fears so they don't rule us. When we reach a calm, confident state of being, we can also think more rationally and logically, which leads to more problem solving.

Modeling this state of being to our kids will not only help them deal with existential threats but with all big situations that will inevitably crop up in their lives.

We cannot expect our kids to reach calm confidence on their own. We owe it to ourselves and our kids to do the inner work, face our fears, and find a way through the anxiety and trauma.

Conscious Parenting Suggestion: Address Your Emotions

Anyone can reach a state of calm confidence. Your only requirement is a willingness to go within, face your emotions, and find a way to deal with them.

Release Emotions

It's okay if you feel afraid, anxious, angry, or any other emotion. There's a lot happening in the world that does feel overwhelming, if not borderline apocalyptic.

Feel it *all*.

That advice may seem counterintuitive to what we sometimes hear from the positive psychology or self-help worlds today. Too often, we're encouraged to focus on the positive. What you focus on, you attract, right? Allowing yourself to feel sad or afraid can trigger feelings of guilt and shame or worry that you'll "attract" the "bad" stuff.

We're here to tell you, nothing you feel is wrong nor should it be denied.

Emotions exist on a spectrum—from happy to sad, from confident to uncertain, from faith to fear. When we refuse to experience all our emotions, we don't stop the negative ones. Instead, we trap our fears and anxieties inside our bodies and minds.

If we don't find a way to release our stuck emotion, it can transform into unresolved trauma, which eventually leaks out physical symptoms and mood swings—irritability, rage, depression, anxiety.

Frankly, if you look at the world and feel anxious or terrified, congratulations! You're being human. It is far healthier for us to meet ourselves where we are.

That means we need to have outlets to express our feelings. This could include journaling, meditating, or talking with your spouse or a friend. It could be going on a long walk, jogging, taking a yoga class, or some other physical activity. It could be painting, drawing, or making music. It could be getting involved or donating to a cause that's working to address the issues that you feel most strongly about.

Some people help to soothe their fears and anxiety through research and learning the facts about an issue. There are amazing people working to address the big issues of today, and finding their stories and work can help remind you of your inner resiliency and of the goodness and kindness of humanity.

If nothing you do seems to help, remember that you can always seek professional help. There's no shame in recruiting allies. A therapist or healer can hold space for you while you process and understand your emotions and can give you tools to manage the uncomfortable moments.

Share Your Feelings

"When something is scary to me, I let my children know," shared Haley Kaijala, a midwife and mother.[1] "I don't want them to think that being afraid is wrong. Fear is fine. It's when fear becomes crippling that it becomes a problem, so I let my children see that Mama is still afraid, but she can work through it and still be their Mama, and still do her job, and live her life."[2]

Allowing our children to see our vulnerability builds their strength. We model for them that fear is normal, and not wrong, and that people can still take action even when they're terrified. It reassures them that it's okay to feel afraid too, instead of worrying about whether that feeling is correct.

We still want to do the solo work to calm down a lot of that fear. We don't want to come off as panicked and amped up on anxiety. Rather, we want to tell our kids, "Yeah, climate change scares me. I care a lot about the environment and the world that you will get to live in. That's one of the reasons we eat less red meat and we've started composting our food scraps. I want to help keep you safe and to make the world safer too."

We won't always say the right things, model the right behaviors, or explain our emotions the right way. That's okay. Our awareness and our attempts to do all of this counts. The more work we do on our emotions and the more we're willing to share our inner journeys and monologues with our kids, the easier it will become.

OVEREXPOSURE TO GRAPHIC IMAGES

Years ago, Dr. Stephen Cowan, holistic developmental pediatrician, worked with a 13-year-old boy who had very severe OCD. During one session, Dr. Cowan was teaching the boy meditation. The boy had become so relaxed and calm, Dr. Cowan was able to ask him what he feared was causing his OCD behaviors.

The boy told him that it was 9/11.

"I asked him if he knew someone who died there," Dr. Cowan told us.[3] "He said, 'No, but so many buildings came down.' I corrected him, explaining that only two buildings had fallen, but the boy was adamant that thousands of them had fallen. I looked at him like he was hallucinating. Then it dawned on me: exposure."[4]

The boy was four years old when 9/11 happened. He saw the image of the Twin Towers falling and people weeping and in shock on replay, and those pictures became fixated in the child's mind.

According to Dr. Cowan, "He got locked in, and trauma got physically locked into him."[5]

While Dr. Cowan admits his patient was an extreme example, the boy's story illustrates the power that moving images on television or devices can have on our children—and the unintended consequences that our 24/7 news cycle can have on our kids.

As a result of the oversaturation of terrible news stories, our kids are developing what Dr. Michele Borba, an educational psychologist and expert on children, teens, parenting, bullying, and moral development, calls *mean world syndrome*. "They're seeing the world as a mean, scary place. What does that do to the child? It builds stress, fear, and it takes down empathy."[6]

No one wants their child to live with mean world syndrome. While we can't stick our kids in a bubble, we can try to limit their exposure. That starts with our awareness. We need to look closely at how much screen time they're getting daily, what kinds of images are coming across their devices, and what we're watching when they're in the room with us.

This doesn't have to be hard or overwhelming. Plugging awareness into our consciousness will automatically help us to start limiting our kids' exposure to violent images on the screen.

Conscious Parenting Suggestion: Manage Exposure

We can't shelter our children from everything, but we can limit some of their exposure, especially at home, while simultaneously reassuring them and helping them to feel safe and secure.

As our kids get older, we can expose them to increasing amounts inside the home. If they are watching stories about a disaster, then we want to make sure we're viewing it with them. That way, we can answer any questions they have, maybe cuddle with them or lean close so they feel safer and we can observe their body language. This allows us to register whether the information they're taking in is too overwhelming. If it is, then we can stop it right away.

It's not just our kids who need to limit their exposure; we do too. We need to find a balance between knowing what's happening in the world without becoming addicted or obsessed with "doom scrolling" about events that drag us down, leave us hating ourselves, each other, and terrified about the world and our futures.

Limiting our news and media to an hour a day can be beneficial, as can taking media breaks. Sign off for 24 hours. Walk away from your devices. Go do something with your family or something community-oriented that reminds you of the "goodness" and hope and light in this world.

COMMUNICATE. COMMUNICATE. COMMUNICATE.

Kids are master storytellers.

They constantly craft stories about the world and themselves, and what's happening and why. But if we don't take an active role in helping them to shape their narratives, they may reach inaccurate conclusions, especially when it comes to disasters and existential fears.

We have to help our kids put huge events into perspective and context, and we have to do it in developmentally appropriate ways that soothe their fears and anxieties, allowing them to be kids— carefree, loving, and fun.

Try to welcome these discussions rather than fear them. It is far better for your child to get the story from you. This is your opportunity to not only give them the true story, but to remind them that they are safe, loved, and protected.

Sometimes we forget about how important those feelings are for kids. If we can help them cultivate this sense of well-being at home, then it will turn into an inner strength that they will carry into the outside world. The earlier you start having these conversations with your kids, the easier they become over time too.

Often, it requires that we dial in to the issues so we have credible facts from credible sources. That may take some research, but it's well worth the time to get the real story before we talk with our kids.

If at any point you feel that your child has developed anxiety beyond what you can comfortably and effectively deal with, seek external resources. There are incredible therapists and experts working with kids of all ages who can help your child process and release whatever fears, anxieties, or possible traumas that have developed.

Conscious Parenting Suggestion:
Meet Your Child Where They Are

At first, it can feel daunting to talk to our kids about serious and complicated issues. Thankfully, it's usually much easier than we fear. Focus on communicating clearly and concisely while leaving them feeling safe and secure, and your child will be off to a good start.

Ask Questions

Instead of guessing where your child lies developmentally, ask them questions that will help clue you in. Say to them, "Tell me about what you think a [insert threat] is," or "What did you hear?" or "What do you know?" or "What did your friends say?"

Their answers will give you a sense of where they're starting, and it will let you correct any misinformation they may have picked up or made up.

Be the Follower

Susie Walton, a parenting educator and teacher and the mother of four sons, shared a remarkable story about a mother whose daughter had her first day of kindergarten on 9/11. Before she took her daughter to school, the mother knew that her husband (the girl's father) was in one of the Twin Towers and that he had probably died.

The mother called her daughter's school and explained the situation. She then asked that no one say a word to her daughter about what had happened. Her daughter was so excited for school, and she didn't want her daughter's day to be ruined.

When her daughter came home and asked about her father, the mother said he was with the angels now and that he would always look down at them. Then she let her child lead the conversation.

"I think it took her daughter until she was about 9 or 10 to know the full story," Susie told us.[7] "When her daughter asked a question, the mother answered it and left it like that. That's my message to parents. Answer a question, whatever it is. Keep it short, and then let your children lead the conversation, whenever that might be. It could be two seconds or two years later, but let them be the leader in those conversations."[8]

Remember: Keep it simple. Concise. And only offer the information they need and can handle.

Be There to Listen

Sometimes the best medicine is a compassionate ear. As Halely Kaijala, a midwife and mother, shared, one of her daughters tends to be more emotional and anxious. When life events come up, they feel bigger to her. Haley discovered that listening to her daughter talk and share her feelings has made the biggest difference.

Our kids need a safe space where they can have all their emotions and aren't judged for what they're feeling or told to stop doing so. The next time you talk with your kid about a fear, let them share how they feel and just listen. Validate that it's okay to feel what they feel and that you understand. Maybe give them a hug and let them know that you're there for them.

You're allowing them to release their fears. Never underestimate the power that comes from being heard and seen.

Create Safety

Part of teaching our children how to handle existential fears is helping them to understand that they and their loved ones are *safe*. "Allowing children to know that it's okay to worry, but then taking the burden from them and saying, 'We will care about this for you, and we will do everything that we can to protect you and keep you safe,' allows them to let go of some of their fears and feel safer," explained Haley Kaijala.[9]

Beyond saying, "You are safe," we want to give our kids concrete examples of what we're doing inside the home and what's happening outside the home. Being prepared for a possible event and sharing with our kids what that means goes a long way toward them feeling safe and secure.

Hank Lutz, a retired major officer who served 27 year in pararescue/combat rescue, recommends using local events as conversation starters. If there is a fire in the neighborhood or smoke in the area from wildfires, then Hank uses these as nonthreatening opportunities to discuss what the family plans look like if something similar were to happen in their own home.

This tactic allows Hank to talk about serious subjects while reminding his children that they are safe and that there are plans in place to make sure they stay that way.

In Hank's home, he also shows his children what's inside medicine kits and how to use the supplies and has them put Band-Aids on each other when one of them gets hurt. This way, they will know to do it automatically in an emergency. "We can't just tell our kids what to do and expect them to do it in these difficult situations," Hank said.[10] "They won't, if they haven't practiced. This doesn't have to be scary; it can be fun."[11]

Teach Self-Care Practices
It is never too early to start teaching our kids how to soothe and take care of themselves. Try introducing some of the following practices and see if they make a difference:

- If your kids are having trouble going to sleep or having nightmares, play calm, instrumental, gentle music in their room—you can do this throughout the day as background music too.

- Read or share happy, inspiring stories.

- Have the kids journal, draw, or use art (depending on their age) to deal with the scary stuff.

- Try aromatherapy, which can help calm anxious children. Some of the most beneficial scents are lavender, peppermint, orange, and ginger. (This should be used for children over the age of five.)

THE COMFORT OF US

We live in a hyper-stimulated culture.

We don't have to go to sleep when it gets dark like our ancestors once did. In mere seconds we can call, text, or video chat with a friend or loved one on any continent in any time zone. We can listen to music or watch movies whenever we want, from wherever. We can drive our cars across the country or hop on airplanes and be across an ocean in hours.

We can have just about anything we want to eat or drink in any season, and we are no longer restricted to our natural cycles.

Yet, for all the improvements in living standards, we have become ungrounded.

We live in a state of hypervigilance—that's fear, anxiety, and stress. That's the state many of our children find themselves in today. Now, pair that with the truth that our kids are inheriting a world that needs a lot of love, care, and consciousness, and it's no wonder that it can be too much for our kids to absorb, process, and understand.

One way to help ground kids and combat their feelings of existential dread is to give them what Dr. Stephen Cowan calls the *comfort of us*. "It's not 'me against the world.' It's, 'we're all in it together. And we're going to figure it out together.'"[12]

As Dr. Cowan shared, he's an optimist because the positive comes from the fact that he knows that humans can figure out all kinds of amazing things when they work together. It only falls apart when it's every person for themselves. By emphasizing to our children that there are amazing, inspiring people working every day to keep them safe and to solve these huge conflicts, we counterbalance the negativity and feelings of hopelessness.

When we show our kids that there are inspiring people working to solve big problems, we also teach them the power of agency. "Trauma happens when kids feel overwhelmed and that their agency is taken away," said Taylor Ross, a trauma-informed parenting consultant and education consultant.[13] "If we keep letting our kids know that this is a scary place and there's nothing anyone can do about it, that's when we're in trouble. But if we let them know there's stuff out there that's overwhelming *and* we have heroes who are working hard to turn this around, that makes a difference."[14]

Giving our kids the "comfort of us" empowers them to see and feel that they are also a member of this extraordinary community of people.

Conscious Parenting Suggestion: Flip the Script from Fear to Empowered Action

When it comes to existential fears, we have two options: (1) worry about them, which is a natural default, or (2) show up to be the very best version of ourselves and teach our kids how to do the same.

Taking action toward a goal or in the direction of change helps to counteract our kids' fears.

Focus on Small Acts

We can teach our children how these experiences may impact their lives, and we can simultaneously show them how their individual choices can help address these big challenges. Take climate change, for example. We can talk to our kids about how our families are making different choices to better care for the environment. We want to share with our kids *how* and *why* we bring reusable bags to the grocery store with us or buy organic, locally raised meats and vegetables, or why we recycle or conserve electricity and water, or why we drive a hybrid or electric vehicle, walk, or use public transit.

Looking for family activities like a beach cleanup, taking litter bags on a hike, or volunteering for a cause can be other ways that show our children positive, empowered actions that they can take right now.

"We're essentially teaching them how to grow up into adults who are paying attention, who are leading the changes that we have to make as humans to either mitigate the effects of these crises or survive them," explained Sarah Nannen, an empowerment coach and mother.[15] "At the very least, it's going to take leadership. It's going to take people paying attention. It's going to take people making what seemed like insignificant changes in their lives to help resolve these struggles."[16]

When we take action and explain why to our children, we're awakening their consciousness at a young age. That's empowering! "The more empowered we can help them feel and help them realize how amazing they are, the better," said Sarah. "They are so much better at this human being thing than we are, actually."[17]

Instill Leadership Qualities

As the father of seven kids, Andrew Marr has dealt with his share of kids' fears. Although his family lives in California and faces their share of potential existential threats, it was the terror of tornadoes that did in one of his daughters. "I wasn't like, 'Hey, this will never happen to us,' but it was educating her on all the realities of tornadoes, and more importantly, how to identify inclement weather that could turn into something more difficult, and then it was teaching her to be a leader," explained Andrew, a retired special forces Green Beret and chairman and co-founder of Warrior Angels, an organization dedicated to helping people in the military to heal from traumatic brain injuries.[18]

Andrew and his wife are open and honest with their children about the difficulties in the world like wars and natural disasters, but they balance that with helping their kids understand what they can control, so they feel empowered instead of paralyzed by terror. They will talk with the kids about what they need to do to be prepared in different situations, how they can identify a situation, and how they can take action to not only take care of themselves, but those whom they care about or maybe can't care for themselves.

"This flips the script from being in a fear mindset to being, 'Okay, it could happen, and if it does, I'll be ready to act,'" said Andrew.[19]

T.A.L.K.

Disasters and significant events can make people, especially our kids, feel powerless. If a big disaster happens, we want to get in front of it with our kids, making sure we're telling them the facts instead of the kid next door. Dr. Michele Borba, an educational psychologist, suggests using her tool *T.A.L.K.* to help us engage with our kids on these sensitive subjects.

T.A.L.K. stands for:

Talk: "Your child needs to hear the news coming from you," said Dr. Borba. "Very often, they hear wrong facts and far more disturbing facts from a friend. Talk, and say to them, 'What are you hearing? What did your friends say?'" These questions help us to understand what our children know and how they see an event.[20]

Assess: Dr. Borba advised to gauge how our children are doing. "Each child is going to handle it [the event] differently. Some kids don't handle it well right away, others seem to handle it well, but two weeks later, they are serious." We need to pay attention to how our kids generally seem. If they seem off, then we need to talk with them and address the event again, remembering to reiterate that they are safe, we are safe, and our family is safe."[21]

Listen: We need to hear what our children have to say about what they've seen and then provide facts and the truth about what happened.[22]

Kindle hope: Disasters are scary and the stories they see or hear may be filled with frightening images. We want to counter that with the positive too. Tell them about all the doctors, first responders, and everyday citizens who are helping to save, fix, and heal the people in trouble. Create balance by offering inspiration.[23]

BECOMING CONSCIOUS

Malcolm knew he needed a different strategy. He called Sam's mother (his ex-wife) and asked if she was fielding similar questions. She was too, but not as much as Malcolm. They talked about bringing him to a therapist or calling his school but decided to first try researching better responses.

Malcolm took the lead and discovered a few techniques to try, which he talked through with his ex-wife and they both agreed to use. First, Malcolm waited until Sam brought up tornadoes again, and instead of immediately telling him that there was nothing to worry about, Malcolm asked Sam, "What do you know about tornadoes?" and "Where did you hear about them?"

Sam's answers were very informative. There had been some devastating tornadoes in the Midwest, and Sam had seen the images on the news, which Malcolm usually turned on after they were done with dinner. To Sam, he believed that when the "bad weather comes, the wind picks up, and it knocks homes over."

Then Malcolm asked Sam what he was afraid of. One of the techniques Malcolm had learned was to let his son talk about his fears. Sam said he was afraid that a tornado would come crashing through the house, knock down all the walls, blow away the roof, and everyone, including their dog, Lola, would get trapped.

"Tornadoes are scary, Sam. Thankfully, we live in a state where tornadoes aren't something that we deal with. Let me show you something," Malcolm said and pulled up a map of the United States on his computer. He showed Sam where they live and how far away they were from where tornadoes usually strike. Malcolm also talked about how people who lived near tornadoes were usually given warnings, so they and their pets could go to their safe rooms that protected them from the storms.

Malcolm had also read that he needed to reinforce that Sam was safe. He explained to Sam that although it was unlikely they'd ever get a tornado, if they did, Malcolm had a family plan. Malcolm and Sam would grab blankets and a flashlight, go with Lola into their basement—where there were no windows—and they would curl up together in a corner to wait out the storm. (If they lived with a constant threat of tornadoes, Malcolm would have put together an actual tornado safety kit.)

Sam seemed very interested in the plan and wondered if maybe they should keep a flashlight in the basement "just in case" now. Malcolm didn't think it was necessary, but Sam seemed into the idea, so Malcolm figured if it eased his son's fears, why not?

He let Sam pick out the flashlight he wanted to keep in the basement, and Malcolm let Sam pick out the spot to store it. Sam decided on the "tornado corner," as he called it.

Then Malcolm told Sam about how tornadoes were created from weather patterns, but Sam didn't seem interested in them any longer. He wanted to play outside. Malcolm left the conversation at that. If Sam wanted to talk more about it later, then he'd bring it up.

The final technique Malcolm tried was limiting the news around Sam. Malcolm had always thought Sam was tuning out the television; he was always playing with his Legos after dinner in the family room. Apparently not. Malcolm decided that he'd wait until after Sam was in bed to turn on the news or he'd just read the headlines on his computer.

Sam still brought up tornadoes to Malcolm, who tried patiently listening to his son, reiterated that he was safe and they had a plan, and answered only the questions Sam had. Overall, Sam's fears never got worse, and his anxieties and fears appeared to lessen.

Conscious Parenting Challenge

Introduce self-care activities. Instead of teaching kids to ignore or stuff their difficult emotions, we want to show them how to cope and release them. Self-care is the way to go. So for one week, we challenge you to introduce a new self-care activity into your kid's daily routine. It can be anything from journaling to drawing, from playing music to running outside, to light age-appropriate yoga, qigong exercises, or deep breathing. We want you to do this with them! That's right, grab a timer and get into it with your kids. As a bonus, ask them how they feel when they're done. Remember, you probably will have to go first, telling them how you feel or what you're thinking as an example.

CHAPTER 5

CONSUMERISM

"We have to do something about this. It's getting out of hand," Kwame said to his wife, Michelle, after the kids had gone to bed.

Kwame and Michelle's kids—nine-year-old Max and five-year-old Jasmin—had so many toys, electronics, and clothes that they had run out of space in their bedrooms, the family room, and the downstairs playroom.

It was October and the couple had been talking about what to buy the kids for Christmas, which became a much larger conversation because they didn't know where they were going to put more stuff.

Michelle had tried to get the kids to give up some of their toys. She had gone through each room with them, holding up small toys, books, puzzles, games, and more stuff that she hadn't seen them play with in months. But her kids hadn't wanted to part with anything. Everything seemed to be special to them, so she didn't push it.

It wasn't just about needing space in the house. Michelle and Kwame were worried that their kids were becoming addicted to buying. Every time they went to a store, the kids would ask for something. These weren't huge requests—a treat, a small action figure, a puzzle.

Kwame and Michelle hated to admit it, but sometimes they would buy things for the kids to avoid a temper tantrum or meltdown, though it was mostly for the simple reason that they liked to make their kids happy.

Both Kwame and Michelle had grown up in blue-collar families, and growing up, they didn't have the popular clothes or toys that a lot of their friends had. They had the extra income and wanted to give their kids something that they hadn't experienced, but they worried that their kids didn't seem to appreciate hard work or value what they had. This made sense because nothing was special. There was no waiting for birthdays or holidays. The kids loved buying and receiving, and Kwame and Michelle worried that their good intentions were instilling the wrong values.

MODERN CHALLENGES

How do we teach our children to value themselves and their possessions when they live in a world driven by consumerism?

This dilemma faces parents everywhere. Having the latest toys, clothes, gadgets, and even foods and drinks can preoccupy our children's minds. They want what they want, in part because the advertising and marketing industry tells them to, but also, they see what their friends have. Wanting the latest and greatest is a rite of passage in childhood. Our kids' desires are not new, but the volume, intensity, and sheer speed at which consumerism gets thrown at our kids is.

Living in a consumer-driven world can leave parents feeling confused and guilty. If you have discretionary spending, it can be difficult to know where to draw the line. Is it so bad to buy your kid a toy on a random shopping trip, or does it harm them to get what they want? If you don't have the extra dollars, then you may worry that your kid is missing out and that you've failed them. Will they be mentally or emotionally damaged because you can't afford the latest toys or clothes like their friends may have?

We know, finding a way through the consumerism maze is a huge challenge for parents, regardless of income levels. Fortunately, it's the same solution for everyone. We teach our kids the meaning of *value*. It doesn't matter how much or how little our kids have; what matters is if they learn how to appreciate, cherish, and care for their possessions. What matters is that we help them to find items that light them up and that bring inner joy to their lives. What matters is that we show them how to value themselves as much, and hopefully more, than they do objects and material possessions.

CONSUMERISM ON STEROIDS

Advertisements target our kids at unprecedented rates and come at them from all directions.

Advertising isn't new. But the mediums used to market products and goods to kids have expanded and built upon each other. It used to be newspapers were the main source, then radios were invented, then television, then cable, then computers and the internet, then social media and streaming devices. And just as our technology is designed to be addictive, the advertising industry purposely and intentionally has turned people into ravenous consumers.

After World War I, corporations needed to ensure they had a population ready and willing to buy the products that companies were overproducing.[1] But at that time, Americans were largely frugal. They bought what they needed when they needed it. Paul Mazur, a banker from Lehman Brothers, realized that if they were going to make money, then the minds and hearts of Americans needed changing.

"We must shift America from a needs, to a desires culture," Mazure said. "People must be trained to desire, to want new things even before the old had been entirely consumed. We must shape a new mentality in America. Man's desires must overshadow his needs."[2]

So it began. Advertising fueled this cultural shift, aided and abetted by Edward Bernays, the nephew of Sigmund Freud, the father of psychology. It was Edward "who showed corporations how to make people want things they didn't need by linking mass-produced goods to unconscious desires."[3]

What are those unconscious desires? To fit in and belong and be liked. To have more or the "right" friends. To fall in love, to be loved. To have wealth and fame. To be thinner, to look young. To have more time in our lives, for our chores—cooking, cleaning, doing laundry—to be easier and more efficient. The list goes on.

In our world today, advertisements have become highly effective thanks to all the data collected from our devices sharing what we search for, where we shop, and what we buy. Specific products get targeted to our likes and desires—and our kids—in ways that previous generations never experienced.

"Part of the reason that advertising works is because it hits on a lack of connection that we have to who we are and what it is that we care about," explained Gabi Jubran, founder and executive director of the nonprofit HAPPI (Helping Awesome Parents Parent Intentionally).[4] "It's based on something that's very surface level and quantifiable that we can change about ourselves to make ourselves feel better, even if it's just temporarily. Advertising feeds into a scarcity mindset."[5]

Our kids are unaware of all of this—and a lot of parents are too. Everyone sees something and they immediately think, "I want that." Our kids are especially susceptible to advertising because they have no defenses against it. Kids are more likely to believe whatever they hear. They don't understand that these advertisements come from a company designed to sell and make money. So our kids see an advertisement and they think, "I am supposed to have that. I need that because I was told I need it."

Very quickly, our kids become trained that the only way to soothe their uncomfortable feelings of "I don't have enough. I am not enough" is to buy more stuff to make them feel okay. But it becomes a terrible self-fulfilling prophecy where they will never buy enough stuff to fill that hole.

We have a window right now where we can equip our children to become critical thinkers about consumerism, toys, and the onslaught of advertising. We can help them understand the difference between their needs and wants and that they are amazing beings not because of what toys and possessions they have acquired, but because of who they are on the inside. They can learn that fulfillment comes from within through the connections we have to ourselves, our loved ones, our communities, and life and nature.

Conscious Parenting Suggestion:
Create Informed Consumers

No one is suggesting that you cease and desist all purchases. There are many products that have made our lives better and easier (hello, laundry machines) and fun (hello, alpine skis and outdoor gear). That goes for our kids too. There are some great science and STEM experiment kits, toys, games, and electronics that we wish we had growing up.

The goal here isn't to get to zero purchases; it's to get to quality. We want our kids to appreciate what they are given or what they may buy with their own money. And we want to ensure that our kids understand what we—as a family—value in life. This will help them become more informed consumers and will give them the skills they need to avoid getting sucked into the advertising vortex as adults.

Differentiate between Need versus Want
In our modern culture, we lack a clear distinction between need and want. All wants, according to advertisers, are needs.

But that's false. In reality, we need very little. If we want our kids to become responsible consumers who buy what they need and indulge in their wants, within reason, then we have to teach them now the difference between a need and a want.

Stacey Robbins, an integrated wellness coach and mother of two, has practiced making this distinction with her sons since they were toddlers. "We would be in a store, and my kids would overhear someone say, 'Oh, I need this,' and they would turn to me and ask, 'Momma, do *we* need this?' I would say, 'No, we don't need that in particular. We *want* that, but we don't need that. We need air or we won't live. We need food and shelter, or we won't survive. We need love in order to thrive. Yes, we need clothes, but which clothes? That's a want.'"[6]

The next time your child asks you for something, try having a need versus want conversation. You may have to lead the conversation and help them to see the differences. That's okay. Kids are sharp. Over time, they'll pick up on it. It may not stop them from asking for things, but you will start to help them develop an important tool they will use for a lifetime.

"Tell Me about the Last Toy You Got"

Kids have, and will, always want more things as they get older—toys, games, electronics, clothes. Laura Kalmes, professor of education at Illinois State University and a mother of three, has an activity she does with her children when they want something new. She asks them a series of questions, beginning with:

- How did you feel when you got the last new toy?
- How do you feel about that toy now?

Laura explained that this exercise usually goes the same way. Her kids respond to the first question by showing a lot of enthusiasm and excitement, but with the second question, her kids usually feel that the toy "is okay."

"I use this point to reflect that everything, eventually, becomes okay," Laura said.[7] "Then I ask them if they think this new toy that they want will also become 'okay.' They start to recognize there is a misalignment between what they think they want and the need they think it will fill, and the actual experience of buying new things that later aren't so special."[8]

This exercise starts the awareness process for your kids. It doesn't mean that they will suddenly no longer want anything (we can wish). But it gets the wheels turning, and it begins conditioning our kids that this "must-have-it-now" item will lose its luster too.

Nix the Commercials and Ads

Like most things in life, we are the primary gatekeepers for our children. And just like we need to pay attention to the content they consume, we need to monitor and reduce our children's exposure to commercials and marketing campaigns. Of course, we can't eliminate everything. Go to the grocery store, and your kid wants a toothbrush that's an ad for the latest superhero movie or some character they've seen in the toy store.

Still, we have the power to limit advertisements in some mediums more than others. This is another reason why you want to be dialed in to what devices and content your kids consume. Try not to leave them unattended watching television or using a computer. If you're with them, then you will see what your kids see.

Some of our experts said they use commercial-free or very limited mediums. Streaming platforms were a popular work-around, which reduces ad content. This may be an option worth considering, if you can.

Another great suggestion from Dr. Michele Borba, an educational psychologist, was *hit the mute button*. "You're watching TV with your child, keep the remote next to you. As soon as the commercial comes on, turn it off. That's your time to talk. You got two minutes for a one on one, and then you can go back to what you were watching."[9]

The commercial break is a small sliver of time you get to ask your kids what they feel or think about the show they're watching, their favorite part so far, and why. You can also share your thoughts and emotions about what you're watching.

You won't raise a commercial-free kid forever. That's impossible. But limiting their exposure will provide some protection to their impressionable young minds and hearts.

Turn the Spotlight on Yourself

What do you buy? How much? How often? What are your purchasing habits telling your kids about life? We need to ask ourselves about our relationships with consumerism too. If we find personal satisfaction in buying lots of products and gadgets and filling our homes to the brim with stuff, then that will influence our kids. If we don't have the means to buy what we want but we talk about it often like "I wish I had . . ." then our kids will pick up on this longing and desire. They will mirror the ways in which we behave and express our wants versus needs.

We have to get honest about what we're buying and consuming in our lives and what we value. That may require us to place limits on what we buy and when.

This isn't to make you feel bad or guilty about what you buy. We all splurge. We have prized possessions and favorite activities that we derive real joy from. No one says you need to deprive yourself.

What we buy is also an opportunity to explain to our kids why we choose to spend money on some items and not others. If you have a hobby you love, use that as a springboard. You can teach your children about what you spend money on and why those things or experiences support your values. Spending money on things that enhance our lives allows for a deeper, authentic expression of our personalities and interests.

We buy with intention. We buy with a purpose. We buy consciously.

DAMAGING THE SELF

Haley Kaijala, a midwife and mother of three, and her husband have intentionally kept commercials and marketing away from their kids. They don't have cable television and they use ad-free streaming devices at home. "I think it's really important that we are very conscious of what our kids are exposed to," she said.[10]

The first time one of her daughters mentioned something about her body was after she saw a commercial. "It was post-Christmas, and I don't know if it was an ad for a workout program, but she saw a commercial at her grandparents' about fitting into the right dress," recalled Haley.

"She came to me and said, 'My belly is kind of soft and fluffy. Should I do something about that?' I'm like, 'You're eight. No.' But she had believed so hard what was told to her."[11]

Welcome to the power of advertisements and our consumer culture. By its design, it focuses us on a perceived "lack" as if there is something "wrong" with us that only their product can fix.

From commercials to the products and toys that get marketed to them, our kids get exposed to unrealistic and unhealthy standards about what their bodies "should" look like. This can damage their self-esteem and self-confidence, and disconnects them from feeling good about themselves and who they are.

Some of our experts expressed concern that the toys kids play with can also undermine their sense of self-worth and self-image. Laura Kalmes, professor of education and mother, explained that she believes some male action figures promote the "ideal" masculine body type as being muscular and toned, while dolls that girls play with may project unrealistic and unhealthy beauty standards. "I have a controversial stance on things like Bratz dolls and Barbies," said Laura.[12] "A lot of people see these as harmless, and girls enjoy playing with them, but if it were a physical toxin, we wouldn't give our kids something poisonous to play with because everybody else is doing it. When it comes to social play, we actively participate in social poisoning of our children. We poison their definitions of their worthiness and what is beauty. We treat toys like they're innocuous because everyone else has them, but they are not innocuous."[13]

No one person can change our consumer-based culture. But at the very least, we can have conversations with our kids about body positivity and how incredible they are as human beings, and we can help them to find activities that increase their self-confidence and self-esteem.

We have to take the issues around toys and consumer products and their impact on our kids' self-esteem and self-confidence seriously. The parts may seem independent, but from the television show they watch to the toy they play with to the cereal box we buy, it's all connected.

Conscious Parenting Suggestion: Boost Self-Esteem and Self-Confidence

As parents, it's on us to help boost our kid's self-esteem and self-confidence. The more we do that, the more prepared our kids will be to face what's out there.

Offer Praise from the Inside Out

Consumerism plays a huge role in influencing and shaping our kids' self-image. We have the power to counter-program our young ones by ignoring the external and focusing on the internal. Instead of commenting on the "cute shoes/dress" or "I love your hair," we instead praise our kids for the values and inner traits that we recognize in them. For instance:

- "I love how kind you are."
- "Gee, that was a really fair thing you did."
- "Wow, you are a really good listener."
- "That is so creative of you."
- "You kept going even when it was hard, and that's very impressive."

We're searching for the real, genuine strength that our kids possess. The more we praise their inner traits, the more likely their stress levels will decrease and their self-esteem will rise. Try to find at least one thing a day to praise that has nothing to do with an external appearance or achievement.

Don't Hide or Encourage Shame

Every kid wants to be liked and accepted, to have friends and to belong. A big part of that is wanting to have what other kids have. But not every child has bundles of toys or the "right" ones. There is nothing wrong with this, whether it's by necessity or by choice. Will our kids be disappointed? Probably, but they can get through it if we talk to them, being as open as we can be about the reasoning behind our decisions and allowing our kids the space to have their feelings.

That was the case for Haley Kaijala, midwife and mother of three girls. "When my daughter entered kindergarten, all these kids had different toys or they talked about what they got for Christmas, or what they did on weekends. My daughter didn't have that. I had to not be afraid to talk about it with her and to tell her that there's nothing shameful about having less than someone else."[14]

It helped that Haley focused her daughter on all the beautiful toys and stuff that she already had, and together they would make lists of all the wonderful things in her daughter's life that made her happy. "I wanted her to find value in her life," Haley explained. "I would talk to her about how not everyone's going to have the same things in life or will value the same things that we do as a family. I acknowledged the differences, and I let her be sad."[15]

Haley has carried this openness forward. When her daughter went into first grade, she came home and wanted a cell phone because other kids had one. "She asked me, 'Why don't I have a phone? Why can't I talk?' and I was like, 'Because you're six, and me and your Papa don't think that six-year-olds should have phones.' She was frustrated, but she said, 'Okay.' I still heard about it, because she was a little kid and didn't fully understand. But I think talking to your kids about what you believe in and why allows them to kind of process their world better and not hold on to feelings that they have of being different from others."[16]

Haley said that this approach has largely worked out for her. Although her kids still want things that the other kids have and will cry when they can't get them, life goes on and her kids are generally happy and well adjusted. "In my job, I see that the parents who communicate well with their kids about why they do certain things tend to have children who behave the best."[17]

As Haley said, "I love being able to talk to my children about stuff, and having them talk to me, because then I know exactly how they feel and I'm able to traverse those issues with them, as opposed to preaching at them."

When it comes to the harmful effects of our consumer culture, having an openness with our kids about the issue can help them make better sense of this world and hold on to their connection to themselves, their families, and their values much more easily.

It's Okay to Say No

As parents, we also have to be courageous enough to recognize how dysfunctional and unhealthy some of the toys and clothes and other items marketed to our kids are.

We can draw the line for our kids, because they'll rarely draw it themselves. Sometimes it means an outright, "No, we're not buying that." Other times, we put limits on how long they can play with a toy or when. We can also talk to them about what the toy looks like and how that toy makes them feel when they see it.

These are tough calls to make, and making them means you love your kids and want what's best for them.

Your intuition is usually spot on. If you feel like something isn't right for your kids, listen to that voice. Trust it.

GENDERED TOYS

We think of toys as fun and only for play. That's true, but it's also through toys and playing that our kids start learning about themselves, their likes and interests, and how they express themselves. Sometimes their toys also influence who they grow up to be and the careers they pursue.

Traditionally, we have labeled toys as "boys'" and "girls'," but as Laura Kalmes, professor of education, explained, sticking with these gender segregated distinctions can undermine efforts at authentic identity representation. "When my sons were born, we got these baby onesies that had sayings like 'Mama's little star/dude/hunk,' then when my daughter was born, it was a tidal wave of pink, ruffles, and ribbons. These are both communicating very explicitly about who our kids are expected to be and become, with no regard to who they are and their unique, distinct qualities as kids."[18]

Many toys and clothing get marketed to kids along gender lines. We see this with colors, where blue is considered a "boy's color" and pink a "girl's color." STEM-related toys, cars and trucks, and muscle-bound action figures get put in the "boy's category," while dolls, kitchen sets, and other domestic-related toys still get targeted to girls. But kids need opportunities to discover their interests and who they are without the pressure of having to censor themselves through their toys because "that's a boy's/girl's toy, so I can't play with it."

As parents, we can encourage our children to develop authentic connections to themselves just by stepping back and evaluating the toys and clothing we expose our kids to and letting them decide if it's something they want to play with. Giving them options that go beyond narrow gender definitions can help kids learn about who they are and what activities they enjoy.

Conscious Parenting Suggestion:
See Toys as Tools for Self-Discovery

Kids are drawn to specific activities and toys as a big part of their self-discovery and expression. If we see toys and games and clothes as tools for helping our kids connect to themselves in honest, authentic ways, then we create an incredible foundation from which they will become adults.

Offer Choices

Last time we checked, adult men like clean clothes, good meals, and to raise kids too. So why is it wrong if a boy plays with a kitchen set, a toy vacuum, or a baby doll? Or so what if your girl likes playing with Legos, rock tumblers, and slime kits?

If we expose our kids to different activities and toys, they will show us what they like to play with or wear. What if we allowed our kids to guide their own choices? What if we let them take the lead (within reason) on what they enjoyed playing with, no matter the label attached?

If that makes you uncomfortable, we do get it. Society has trained us and corporations have reinforced the stereotypical toys and clothes that a girl or boy "should" have. Think of this as an experiment and see what happens when you let your child lead based on their likes and personalities and interests.

You may find that this one relatively simple adjustment may result in a happier, more fulfilled, and more interested kid.

BECOMING CONSCIOUS

Kwame and Michelle realized they needed a strategy to deal with the overwhelming toy situation in their home. It also meant they needed to be on the same page as parents to provide consistency.

First, the couple decided they were going to start talking about needs versus wants when the kids asked for something. At first, the kids were confused, but they quickly caught on when Kwame or Michelle explained the differences.

Next, Kwame and Michelle sat the kids down and told them that since Christmas was approaching, they needed to make space in their rooms for new toys. "We're going to pick out the toys you no longer play with, and then we're going to give them away so kids who don't have them will have something to play with too,"

Michelle said. The kids pushed back like they had done the first time with Michelle, but Kwame and Michelle stayed unified.

Kwame and Michelle made a game of it too. Each paired off with a child and a garbage bag. "We have thirty minutes to collect all the toys you no longer play with," Kwame said. "It's a race to see who finishes first."

The kids actually seemed excited. It took some prodding from Kwame and Michelle, who said if they hadn't played with something in the last six months, it was a goner, but in the end, the kids did clean out their rooms. They still had a lot of stuff, but it was a start.

Kwame and Michelle also talked about the kinds of toys and games they wanted to buy the kids for Christmas and in the future. Michelle had pointed out that they often bought the kids the bright, shiny toys that looked fun, but after a day or two—maybe a month if they were lucky—the item ended up at the bottom of a chest.

Michelle and Kwame decided to focus more on buying quality items that they knew their kids truly loved that would help them grow and learn too. For Max, that meant more outdoor and STEM activities—a marble maze, a 101-experiment kit, and a miniature garden kit. For Jasmin, it meant dress-up, arts and crafts, Legos, a doctor's outfit complete with a medical bag, and a fairy garden kit.

The couple had thought paring back would be difficult—it wasn't. It was fun and it felt even better to know that they were bringing more balance into their kids' lives instead of feeling like their toys and possessions were running them. Kwame and Michelle still bought the occasional toy or treat for their kids when they were out shopping, and they would still bring popular toys into the mix. It wasn't all-or-nothing. But they made these exceptions rather than the rule.

Conscious Parenting Challenge

Practice saying no. If it's not a birthday, holiday, or special occasion, try saying no the next time your kids ask you for a toy, game, or candy. We know how it feels to watch your kids get excited and to know you gave that to them by saying yes. But we can overdo it. Instead, we want to bring balance and appreciation into our kids' lives so they value and cherish what they do have. For at least one week, preferably longer, flex the no muscle by saying no to all their wants. It may be uncomfortable for you and them, but your kids will move on. It's okay for them to feel disappointment too. In fact, allowing them to feel disappointed teaches them a valuable lesson: there's nothing to fear with uncomfortable feelings.

CHAPTER 6

EDUCATION

Stacey knew she wanted to homeschool her children, even before she became a mother.

Growing up in New Jersey, Stacey had a great public-school experience. Her mother called her "typhoid Mary," because Stacey would go to school no matter how sick she was. That's how much she had loved her teachers and schooling experience, despite having been on the receiving end of a bully—something she never wanted her children to face.

When Stacey was in her twenties, she was a professional musician who performed on stages, in clubs, and in hotels. During this time, she was also a music specialist in a private school, where she fell in love with how community- and mission-oriented the school seemed to be.

Because of health complications, Stacey had been told she would never have children, but she and her husband, Brian, went on to have two boys. As her eldest was nearing school age, Stacey spent time researching, studying, and reading about homeschooling and reflecting on the pros and cons of the public and private school systems.

While Stacey had an excellent public-school experience growing up, looking at the culture through a parent's lens, she wasn't sure it was right for her kids. She disliked the overemphasis on grades and workload; the lack of play; the shortened recess; the elimination of spending time in, and exploring, nature; and how much bullying takes place and how mishandled it often is.

Stacey had an ideal for her sons that couldn't be found in the public—or private—setting. Stacey wanted to share life with her children, watch them grow, get to know them as individuals, and help them cultivate their strengths and gifts.

Brian didn't have as strong of a feeling about where their kids went to school as Stacey did. The neighborhood school that their boys would attend was where Brian had gone as a kid, and he liked his experience too. Brian believed their sons would thrive no matter what school they attended.

But he also recognized how strongly his wife felt about home-schooling, and if that was something she wanted to try, then he'd support her and the boys in whatever ways he could.

As the months passed and Stacey spent more time researching and reflecting on homeschooling, the more convinced she became that it was the right road for them, but could she shoulder all of that responsibility? Should she? Would she deprive her boys of the wonderful public-school experience that she had? Would they miss out on the friendships and important socialization with their peers? And what about the amazing private-school community and mission-mindedness she saw when she taught music? Would her sons thrive more in one of those environments instead?

Stacey had so many questions, but she knew there would be no answers unless she tried homeschooling. However, as much as she wanted to take the plunge, Stacey was also terrified of failing and setting her kids back.

MODERN CHALLENGES

Education has changed a lot in the last few decades.

Just look at the school building for example. Many schools today have huge fences around the buildings and yards, designed to pro-tect kids from mass shootings. Next, try walking into the building. You can't just go through most doors. You get buzzed in and have to present your license so that officials know who you are. You may also see armed security officers and surveillance cameras cover the halls and grounds.

Our kids have armed-shooter drills, just like the fire, earthquake, and bomb drills some of us may have grown up with. They walk by posters about tutoring, test preparation, and who to call for extra support, on top of the hours of homework they probably had to grind through the night before. Then there are the notices and conversations about signs of depression, suicide awareness, and where to go for help if they or their friend needs it. That's not a new topic; suicide among kids, especially teens, has sadly been a reality for decades. But what's unique is the frequency that suicide and its ripple effects are having on our youth today.

For our kids, it's not one thing, but the stacking of these issues that has created a very different environment and culture that our kids are learning and growing in from when we were growing up. This change means that many kids are experiencing more anxiety and stress, so when they come home from school, they need us to recognize their worlds, and to stay cool, calm, and collected.

At the same time, to ensure our kids come out healthy, well rounded, and get the best education they can, we have to get involved. We're not talking about becoming a "helicopter" or "tiger" parent, but spending time at night with them when they're learning how to read, or going over their homework with them, or helping to instill habits and behaviors about meeting deadlines and doing their best, and encouraging the development of their talents and skills.

Maybe this sounds exhausting or you don't know how you'll find the time to spend with them when you barely have a moment to breathe. Most parents are already working hard to raise well-rounded kids, provide for their families, and take care of everyone's needs. The last thing we want to do with this chapter is make it feel like "one more task" that will overload you or make you feel like your child will be doomed if you "screw this up" or you don't get them into the "right program."

Instead, we want to help you see education through your child's eyes, and to feel inspired and excited about helping them to learn. Kids are born learners. They want to discover the world. They seek to find patterns. They have unique interests that light them up. Education comes through many channels, and yes, we want our kids to do well in school, and we want to help them find their passions, identify their talents and gifts, and develop the skills they need to thrive as adults. This can be fun for them and for you. When you find the areas that your kid genuinely loves, you will see their joy, excitement, and focus. You can help them tap into these interests, with or without formal schooling. There is nothing more empowering that you can instill and encourage in your child than a passion for learning.

THINK BEYOND TEST SCORES

Gabi Jubran, founder and executive director of the nonprofit HAPPI (Helping Awesome Parents Parent Intentionally), did what she had to do to get by when she was in school. "I wasn't good at science or math, so I accepted that I wasn't smart. I faked it until I got out of school, and that was damaging to me. I didn't know that I had social and emotional intelligence off the charts—I didn't even know that was a thing. I intuitively did it and enjoyed connecting with people and understanding their stories and learning more about them."[1]

It wasn't until Gabi started teaching herself how to dance that she started to realize she might actually be good at something. It took finding something that she cared about for her to experience the joy of learning.

This relatively simple realization transformed Gabi's world. She is happy and thriving and successful today and has had a happy ending, but imagine if she could have discovered this earlier in life. Imagine if she could have had a more positive experience growing up. Imagine if she had believed in her intelligence. Now, imagine how many kids like Gabi walk through the world but never learn what she did.

Over the last few decades, education has gone haywire by pairing standards with aggressive testing preparation. Authentic, organic learning—the aha and joy and enthusiasm—has been exchanged for rote memorization and becoming a good test taker.

Granted, we understand. Test scores matter for schools. Having a standard expectation for what kids learn in each grade is important. It's how they get funding. Without them, every state and local school would be wildly different. But they narrow our education and don't tell the full picture.

"A child with strong test scores is meeting the relatively mediocre demands of the state educational system, but that doesn't mean they have developed the intellectual, imaginative, or self-control types of behaviors that we know predict real achievement and a happy professional life," said Heather Miller, who owns and directs an education company that produces educational programs used in schools.[2]

"They're helpful because we need to know where a child is, more or less, as a reader and as a mathematician, but scores don't tell us anything about things like follow-through stamina, long-term concentration, the ability to do steps in a process; they don't tell us that much about curiosity or about a child's ability to work with others. These are the very things that make people successful."[3]

As parents, it's easy to put a lot of pressure on our kids to earn top grades. Susie Walton, a parenting educator and teacher, explained what she did with her firstborn. "I was so bad, I would say stuff like, 'With your potential, if you just did your homework, you'd have a 4.0,' and he was like, 'Why? I already know this stuff.' It was true. I was just on him all the time, and it wasn't good because I paid more attention to the grades than I did other elements like he was very disciplined in class, very cooperative, he never messed around, and was a perfect student for teachers."[4]

As Susie realized, "It's not all about the grades; it's about the person and the life lessons our kids learn in class."[5]

Pause for a moment and think about how much you remember from school. It's probably a small percentage. It wasn't so much the dates or periodic table of elements you memorized; it was the lifelong values that you gained. School teaches us how to commit to getting something done on time, how to listen and follow directions, how to be respectful to the teacher and classmates, how to work together, and how to problem solve.

"I always tell parents, when your kid goes off to get a job, I doubt their employer is going to ask for their eighth-grade report card," explained Susie. "They're going to ask about the person. We're finding more these days that owners of companies are looking for people that are more well-rounded and not just ultra-focused on one subject. It's about the whole person."[6]

To be clear, this isn't a pass for kids to "do whatever" in school or to not care about their grades. Rather, it's about awakening to a broader perspective and understanding that grades matter *to an extent*, but they aren't everything.

All of the experts we spoke to talked about the systemic challenge in education today: it doesn't fully prepare children for a career in a world that continues to rapidly change. "There's this predicament with standardized education," explained Laura Kalmes, professor of education.[7] "What our kids need more than content and area expertise in just the sciences, social sciences, and mathematics is for them to be equipped with the capacity for critical thinking and self-learning. In many ways, standardized education is contrary to critical thought and independent learning. This is where schooling is potentially quite dangerous to the process of learning the necessary things that children need to become productive members of society and to become healthy, functional adults."[8]

Instead of allowing the system to determine if our kids are "smart" or if they'll be "successful," the most important thing we can do is throw up a stop sign.

If our kids struggle with test scores, we have the power to see them and reinforce to them that they are smart. Maybe they aren't good test takers. Maybe the school setting, where they have to sit for eight hours a day with very little exercise and physical movement, doesn't work for them.

Go with us here for a second. What if our kids don't need us hounding them about their grades and pressuring them to succeed based on an outdated education model? Instead, what if they need us to lighten up and release them from the burden to perform and succeed based solely on test scores or a grade on a report card?

What if what our kids need most is for us to see their intelligence, wherever it may lie, and support them in gaining skills and nurturing their natural talents?

Our kids need us to see their value, worth, and potential beyond a test score. Even those kids who get straight As and who ace their exams need us to recognize that they are more than a number. By separating our kids, their worth and value, their skills and talents, from a test score, we set our kids free.

Conscious Parenting Suggestion: Focus on Preparing Kids for the Future

Some people believe in changing a system. Others believe in finding ways to thrive within the existing structure. If you feel compelled to take up the education transformation banner, then go for it. If not, then don't despair. There is hope. It comes from catching the work-arounds, shifting your focus, and helping your kids prepare both inside and outside the system.

"Children are born to learn, it's in their DNA," explained Laura Kalmes.[9] "Children develop very dysfunctional relationships to the institutionalized nature of schooling and the very prescriptive top-down standardized experience they have, but no child has a dys-functional relationship to learning."[10]

As parents, we can help our kids embrace the joy of learning by broadening our definitions of what "being smart" means. For a moment, let's try to forget about the test scores and just look at our kid with clear vision. What are their strengths? What are their talents? What are they so good at that we shake our heads in awe? What lights them up? What interests them?

These are the questions that can help us identify our kids' innate intelligence, which we can then praise and support. Let's show them we're excited for them. For some kids, math and science lights them up. It's as if they were born understanding these subjects. Other kids have an innate ability to build and use their hands to create. Some kids have physical prowess. Others have empathy and compassion off the charts. Some kids love nature and exploring the natural world. Others are incredible artists or creators.

It takes a wide swathe of talents and intelligence to keep our world turning—and that's a good thing.

Help your child find their genius. Praise, encourage, and chal-lenge them to embrace their intelligence and be open to where it may take the both of you.

IS HOMESCHOOLING THE ANSWER?

There's a lot of chatter about homeschooling today.

The flexibility in how, where, when, and to some extent what kids learn have driven parents to take the leap and take on the role of teacher too.

With homeschooling, you can customize and tailor the curriculum, although there are state standards that your child has to meet. Many homeschooling advocates note the different enrichment opportunities they can provide to their kids, including museum tours, cultural experiences, spending more time in nature, and being more creative and pursuing the arts.

Robin Ray Green, a licensed acupuncturist, pediatric acupuncture expert, and mother who homeschools her children, has also experienced emotional advantages from homeschooling her kids. "You're with them so often, and you're guiding them in such a way that you form a deeper bond and relationship with your children. As they become teenagers, they're going to want to separate themselves from you, but it's not in a way that becomes defiant. You see them become these independent-thinking young adults, and it's really beautiful."[11]

Robin has made it a point to connect with other homeschooling parents in her area so her kids and theirs can interact too. What she's found is that some of the social pressures that kids often face have disappeared or seemed easier to resolve. "There are going to be issues and conflicts that arise, which are natural when kids are in school," Robin explained.[12] "I found as a homeschooling parent that I knew the other homeschooling parents, so it felt like we were able to guide our kids better through resolving conflicts because we knew each other."[13]

But before you yank your kid out of school and begin a homeschooling adventure, we have to share the other side too. Like everything in life, there are pros and cons. "I mostly see that a desire to control what a child is learning is what prompts homeschooling, but there are many grave problems with it," shared Heather Miller.[14] "In traditional school, children have to learn how to work with others; how to make friends; how to repair friendships when they go wrong, as they always will; how to get projects completed with other people; how to deal with people they don't like or people who don't like them, and to be able to cope in ways that doesn't devolve into outright aggression or misery. These are incredibly important skills of a civilized person."[15]

As Heather explained, it's difficult to teach these skills when we homeschool. "It's not enough to put them on a sports team and think that that's going to get the job done. If you're on a sports team, you're already selecting that group for having a common interest, and it's not a six-hour experience. The way that school is every single day, you really need to have that kind of regular exposure to a group of people who you haven't chosen, and who you have to get along with in order to socialize."[16]

Another downside to homeschooling is that parents spend *a lot* of time—think 24/7—with their children. That can be challenging and frustrating for everyone.

Children still need outside experiences and interactions with other people and kids that go beyond their parents and family units. To counteract that, parents have to proactively seek out and arrange for other people to be included in their kids' learning environments. Robin Ray Green recruits people to come in and advise, and sometimes teach, her kids other subjects. This gives her kids space from her and a chance for them to interact and learn from other people. It has worked for Robin and her boys, but it takes effort on Robin's part to make this happen.

Which raises the biggest hurdle: the tremendous responsibility that homeschooling places on parents, or at the very least, one parent, who stay at home teaching. Homeschooling is not for the faint of heart. It's *work*.

Which is probably why Heather Miller said that most homeschooling she's seen becomes a temporary experience, as opposed to a multiyear adventure.

Is homeschooling good or bad for your children? That depends on you, them, your homelife, and situation. It's not something to enter into lightly, nor is it something to discount fully. The experts we spoke with who have also homeschooled their kids have had very positive experiences. Some parents have had their children take a break from external education to be homeschooled for a year or two, after which the kids reenter traditional school.

Conscious Parenting Suggestion: Connect Kids and Curiosity

"Follow your kids' lead, follow their curiosity, and they will learn," said Laura Kalmes, who has homeschooled her kids at different ages.[17] "It's hard to prevent a kid from learning when they're curious about something. Our task ought to be to connect them with their own curiosity."[18]

We don't have to homeschool our kids or wait for the education system to do this. We do this at night, on the weekends, in the mornings. We pay attention to what our kids seem excited by. We expose them to different areas and activities to see what they gravitate toward. We give them opportunities to learn by walking beside them in life, showing, teaching, and exploring with them.

If you let go of the reins a little on "what they should learn" and instead let them show you what opens their mind and heart, you may be amazed at what you discover together.

THE REALITY OF BULLYING

We can't leave the education conversation without addressing bullying. It's a problem. It's always been a problem, and it's escalating.

Before the internet and social media, kids could be shielded more when they went home. But the emotional abuse that can happen to our kids now travels with them. "Bullying is more intrusive, hurtful, and damaging because kids are so connected to their devices, they can't get away from it," explained Reena B. Patel, a child and educational psychologist who specializes in behavior.[19]

Bullying can happen at all ages, but it ramps up and gets more vicious in middle school. This is the point when children's brain development gives them a larger sense of the world and where they may, or may not, fit into it. "Kids begin to perceive that, in some sense, life is a contest or, at least, school is, and they may not be winning it," shared Heather Miller.[20] "They start engaging in behaviors to try to push themselves up."[21]

"Parents often think bullying is a kid being a little mean, but bullying has three parts," shared Dr. Michele Borba, an educational psychologist and expert on bullying.[22] "The first part: it is always intentional. It's never an accident. It's purposeful. Second, it's cold-blooded meanness, where the child is deliberately picking on another child. And the third is that there's a power imbalance. A child who's picked on or bullied can't hold their own."[23]

As Dr. Borba explained, there are four types of bullying:

1. **Face to face.** When a child verbally taunts, picks on, and makes other horrific, mean, shameful comments to another child.

2. **Physical.** This is slamming, pushing, dunking, hitting, stealing, or another physical act.

3. **Deliberate exclusion.** "You can't sit with us. Go over there," is an example of how children intentionally leave someone out.

4. **Cyber bullying.** This happens over text, email, or on social media and has become more prevalent as kids use technology more.

Many parents have bullying on their radar screens, but it's a complex issue. Kids often hide being bullied from their parents. We have to pay attention to the subtle signs that our child is being bullied, open the lines of communication, make sure they feel loved and supported and that they have an ally in us, and ensure they know we will do everything we can to help them feel safe at school.

And if we're parents of the bully, then we have to be able to accept that, do some honest soul searching about our behaviors or what our child has been exposed to, and course-correct with our kids so they know that this behavior is absolutely unacceptable.

A power imbalance lies at the heart of bullying. Bullies are typically insecure, feeling like they must grab power from someone who they perceive as being weaker. We cannot expect our kids to grow past being a bully—or a victim—without our help and guidance.

"As a culture, we need to heal from how we treat each other," said Stacey Robbins, an integrated wellness coach and mother.[24] "We have to stop being so surprised at the bullying that exists in the school, and we need to start recognizing the bullying that exists in our conversations with each other, with people we don't agree with or who are different from us, and how we treat each other on social media and platforms.[25]

"The way we're going to heal the bullying in the schools is by starting with us and healing our inner critic, that judgmental, harsh person inside of us, and healing the way we converse with each other," said Stacey.[26] "The greatest illusion I think we live in is that we're disconnected, and the greatest truth that we need to come to is that we're all one. When we do this, then we won't see bullying anywhere."[27]

We couldn't agree with Stacey's sentiments more, and we still have to deal with the very real situations that arise for our children. As painful and challenging as these experiences can be, there is hope and healing on the other side. There is learning and growth, and by guiding your child through any bullying experiences, you can help to awaken more inner confidence, assertiveness, and compassion for themselves and others.

Conscious Parenting Suggestion: Be Proactive

The experts we spoke to shared some of their top tips and strategies for parents dealing with bullying.

How to Tell if Your Child Is Being Bullied
There are few experiences more heart-wrenching for parents than learning their child is being bullied. Sometimes finding this out takes serious detective work. "Don't assume that your child is going to come to you and tell you," warned Dr. Borba. "You need to watch for a change in your child's behavior."[28]

Dr. Borba suggested using what she called the *Too Index*. "Every kid's going to have a bad day, but is it *too* often?"[29]

According to Dr. Borba, there are a few telltale signs that can help us determine if our kid is being bullied.

- **They run into the home after school and immediately have to use the bathroom.** Forty-three percent of American kids are afraid to use school restrooms because bullying doesn't happen everywhere; it happens where there's least likely to be adult supervision.

- **They run into the house famished.** That could be a sign that someone is taking their lunch or they don't feel safe enough to eat at lunch.

- **They don't want to go to school and come up with reasons to stay home.** They pretend to be sick or injured. They may stop wanting to participate in after-school activities or want to get home as quickly as possible. They may seem depressed or withdraw from engaging with the family. "It's not that they're walking around crying or showing how unhappy they are, but they're blah," explained Heather Miller. "A blah child with low affect is the thing to really watch for. This is a child who doesn't give much one way or the other."

- **They're not telling you well about what's happening at school.** Typically, there are four reasons for this. The first, Dr. Borba explained, is that most kids feel humiliated and embarrassed. The second is that when kids have told their parents, their parents didn't believe them. "Believe them when they tell you," said Dr. Borba. "If you don't believe them the first time they come to you, then they won't come to you a second time."[30] The third reason kids don't tell their parents about bullying is because parents may have given them bad advice before. Dr. Borba said that many parents will say, "Don't worry about it. It'll get better." But the bullying doesn't get better, so kids stop going to their parents because they see their parents as unhelpful. The fourth reason kids don't talk about bullying is that they're worried about retaliation. When parents learn what's happening, a natural instinct is to say, "I'm going to talk to that bully's parent. I'm going to give them a piece of my mind," and immediately the kid is scared to death because the bullying will get worse.

What to Do if Your Child Is Being Bullied

First, stay calm. Easier said than done, we know, but you want to be calm and confident here. Next, sit with your kid. Be grateful and thank them for telling you, and acknowledge how hard and painful this must be. "If your child is being bullied, you really need to step up the amount of explicit love that you're giving that child at home," shared Heather Miller. "Hugging, saying wonderful things to them about how much you love them, how wonderful they are being, what wonderful specific qualities you see in them—this matters a lot and can mitigate the bullying to an extent."[31]

When they're bullied, many kids believe they've done something wrong or they're asking for it. They haven't. Bullying is about the other kid. We need to do everything we can to make sure our child knows they have done nothing wrong, and that they are not wrong. We need to listen and validate their feelings.

We also need to understand what's happening so we can develop a response plan for our children. Every child deserves to have safe spaces. School should be a safe space and, if need be, we, as their parents, need to help create it.

As you're sitting with your child, ask them:

- **What is happening?** This may be difficult for your child to tell you and for you to hear, but you want to encourage them to share what form of bullying is happening.

- **Where did it happen?** "If you know where bullying is happening, say at the back of the bus, then you can have your kid's seat moved to the front of the bus, on the right-hand side where the bus driver can look," explained Dr. Borba.[32]

- **What time does it happen?** If the bullying happens in the bathroom, suggest to your child that they get a friend to walk with them and go between classes or ask for a pass from the teacher during class when the bathroom will be empty.

- **Who is doing the bullying?** It's almost always the same kids who do it.

These three questions will help you find the pattern because bullying usually happens at the same time, in the same place, by the same kids.

Now you can help your child create a safety net by coming up with alternatives for them like walking a different way or finding another adult or caring person like a friend to buddy up with. "Don't promise your child that it's going to work tomorrow," cautioned Dr. Borba.[33] "Do promise that you will never give up until your child feels safe. And there's going to be a time when you, the parent, has to advocate and say, 'This is getting too difficult, too painful; let's go and talk to your teacher or principal together,' or 'I'll go do the talking.' You need to be the advocate."[34]

What to Do if Your Child Is the Bully

Bullying is a learned behavior that can be unlearned, but it takes parents stepping up to the plate ASAP. "The first time you ever see your child doing anything that's mean or vicious, stop them immediately or it will escalate," said Dr. Borba.[35] "We're seeing too much escalation because we're not stepping in at the very beginning."[36]

It can be hard to accept that your kid is the bully. But as Dr. Borba said, "The greatest advice to a parent of a bully is please believe someone who says that your child is being aggressive."[37] Kids act differently at home, so we want to listen carefully to what someone says.

Then we want to sit with our child and use very strong, empathy-based messages. Here are some questions and directions we can use with our kids, according to Dr. Borba.

- How would you feel if that happened to you?

- What do you need in order to feel better?

- Let's think of your friend. What does your friend need to feel better? How would you feel if you were that friend?

The last piece is that you, as their parent, need to help create a safety net for the other child that has been on the receiving end of your child's abuse. That means telling your child, "You will not mess with that child anymore. You will not play with or engage with that child unless you can treat them fairly, nicely, and kindly, and if they agree to playing and engaging with you again."

We need to back this up by engaging other adults who are likely to be in the area where your child and the other kid interact. That could be a teacher, a daycare provider, or a babysitter. We need to explain what's happening and ask for their help in monitoring your child's behavior. As Dr. Borba said, we can also ask for support in acknowledging your child when they are acting kind and good. This will reinforce the behavior that you're looking for.

Dr. Borba also suggested, "You have to dig deeper and figure out why this behavior is happening, because that's how you raise a strong, healthy, and happy kid."[38]

If that means investing in outside help with a therapist or psychologist who can help unpack what's happening with your child, then please, do it.

Be Honest about Your Behaviors

If our child is acting as a bully, it means we, as parents, need to take an honest look at our actions, behaviors, and environment too.

What's happening in our household? Is bullying taking place? Is sarcasm being used in a cruel way? Is one person in the family ordering other people around in a way that could be described as bullying? Is mocking happening? Is someone putting other people down? Is someone afraid of someone else in the home? Is one parent bullying another parent?

"Bullying is not a particularly natural part of human behavior," said Heather Miller. "In families where there's kindness, gentleness, love, encouragement, and support, you don't see those children bullying."

Bullying may not happen directly in our homes. It could happen outside. Maybe we bully a taxi driver or waiter, or people who we perceive as having less status than we do. It could be that we bully employees or direct reports or colleagues at work. "In my experience, bullying behaviors are very tied to whatever is going on at home, and children pick up on this," said Heather.

Before we can expect our child to change, we have to change. As conscious parents, it means having the strength and courage to admit our own behaviors and then changing them. That's where real power exists.

We can choose to act with more kindness. We can choose to act more compassionately, to develop more patience and gentleness and acceptance. This may mean we seek outside counsel and help. Again, there is no shame and there is nothing wrong with this.

We have the ability to change our trajectory and our children's trajectory, if we choose.

BECOMING CONSCIOUS

Stacey took the plunge and homeschooled her sons for three years. To her delight, she loved it and so did they. They spent time exploring outside, reading books that the boys picked out, researching topics like outer space, playing, and doing art and music. Her boys were young, so everything was age appropriate and Stacey was shocked by how many materials, suggestions, and support groups she found online and in her local community. There were more families homeschooling their kids than she had realized, and she regularly organized outings and teaching swaps with other parents who came to teach her boys while she taught theirs.

Stacey was committed to homeschooling her sons until a health crisis struck her. Stacey could no longer keep up with her boys' lessons. She knew she couldn't serve her kids and teach them the way that they were hungry to learn.

Stacey had a lot of mixed feelings. To her, she was failing an ideal, and putting her kids into public school didn't speak to her. Even so, she needed to pour her energy into healing herself and getting better so she could be the mom and wife she wanted to be.

Trying to find clarity, Stacey went on a long walk. While she was not a very religious person, she was spiritual, and she heard a sentence run through her: "If it's good for you, it's good for them." She felt that what she needed mattered too, not just what the boys needed, and that right now, what she needed most was to heal and to focus on her health. Her intuition told her that her boys would be okay in public school, and that, in fact, it's what they needed.

Stacey and Brian talked, and they decided to enroll the kids in the public elementary school that was within walking distance to their home—the one Brian had attended when he was growing up.

Her kids went for a year, and they had some incredible experiences with great teachers. They had some challenges too, but it worked out overall. During that time, Stacey had decided to apply to a Waldorf school, which the boys were accepted to. At the end of the school year, the boys transferred and had a great community with a lot of diversity in ethnicity, culture, and ideological backgrounds.

Stacey and Brian's boys stayed at the private school for a few years, until Stacey decided to homeschool her kids again. This was for a few reasons. One, her health had turned around and she had the energy and ability to do it. Second, her oldest son had a terrible bullying situation that the school had mismanaged and mishandled, leaving him with trauma and PTSD so bad that he couldn't sleep at night.

All Stacey and Brian wanted was for their son, who was 12 at the time, to heal and feel safe again, and they believed homeschooling could hold that key. And so, back to homeschooling the boys went.

It became a huge turning point in everyone's lives.

Because of the freedom that homeschooling often provides, Stacey arranged a "magical healing adventure." She introduced her eldest to yoga. She went through healing rituals designed to help him talk and release his pain. And she and Brian booked one-way plane tickets to Europe for her and the boys, where they spent three months traveling through different countries, going to museums, visiting foreign cities and towns, eating different food, and allowing their minds and hearts to open—and for her oldest, to heal. She also taught her sons that they could be creative during hard times and had them pour their emotions and experiences into music, painting, and writing—whatever medium called to them.

Stacey saw education as being everywhere for her sons. She still adhered to their state requirements for homeschooling education, but she used life and their experiences to enhance their education. It was a powerful year filled with much healing and learning lifelong skills. And Stacey's eldest emerged having found an inner strength and power within himself.

As the year wound down, Stacey and Brian asked the boys what they wanted for their next school year. They wanted to keep homeschooling, and Stacey wanted to keep teaching them too, so they continued on that track, which they've been on for over five years.

At the end of each year, the family has reevaluated what the best type of schooling would be for them. "There is no perfect place—not at the public school or the private school or in homeschooling—but you choose a situation that's worth whatever trouble there will be," Stacey said.

Stacey's kids, who are now 17 and 15, love learning. They are caring and empathetic, strong and confident.

Conscious Parenting Challenge

Let's try broadening our definition of *smart*. Grab a pen and some paper and make a list of their strengths, talents, and skills. Note their personality and inner traits—are they generous, kind, thoughtful, clever, creative? Record their favorite activities and what they would do for hours if you let them. Jot down what they're good at. Once you have a broad picture, try picking one trait, skill, strength, or activity that you can praise them for. Do this for one week and try to notice any changes in your child's behaviors, attitudes, expressions, and demeanor.

CHAPTER 7

TOXINS

Clint and Bree were scared.

Their son, Aiden, was only five years old, yet he had spent his young life in and out of the hospital. Doctors didn't know what caused Aiden's chronic ear and adenoid infections and had him on antibiotics every other month. Aiden suffered from respiratory issues, painful abscesses, and chronic tonsillitis so badly that one doctor said he had never seen tonsils so swollen on a kid Aiden's age.

Watching their son get poked and prodded while being unable to explain to him what was going on left Bree feeling incredibly guilty. She would cry, wondering what she could do better or what she was doing wrong that was making her baby so sick. Aiden was her first child, and no parenting book that Bree read had prepared her for this. Clint would tell her not to blame herself, that she was a great mother, and that Aiden's illnesses weren't anyone's fault.

There were a few harrowing times when Aiden almost died. There was the time when he ran a 105-degree fever despite being on days of antibiotics. Bree and Clint brought him back to his pediatrician, who prescribed a different antibiotic. The doctor told Bree and Clint that in 12 hours Aiden would be better, so they brought their little guy home.

But his fever didn't break. Bree and Clint were sitting with Aiden in the living room when he walked over to pick up a toy. He took three steps back to Bree and collapsed. The terrified parents strapped Aiden in his car seat and took off for the hospital. It turned out the abscesses and the multitude of infections had taken their toll on his little body.

Then there was the time he went in for surgery to have his tonsils removed. He ended up with complications and stopped breathing. Stuck in a code-blue situation, doctors and nurses raced into his recovery room and whizzed him up to the ICU.

One stint at the children's hospital lasted about five weeks. When the doctors finally released him, they told Bree and Clint that his immune system had become so compromised that Aiden needed to be secluded and isolated from everyone. No going to the grocery store or seeing anyone outside of his parents for at least a month.

As Aiden got ready to start kindergarten, Bree and Clint discovered another challenge: wearing clothing. When Aiden put on or pulled off clothes, or if he had to wear layers or anything that added a little extra weight, he'd scream, "It hurts! It hurts!"

Bree and Clint had no idea what was happening, and none of Aiden's doctors did either. So the parents tried work-arounds for their son. They tried to find material that felt okay to him, and they allowed him to wear as few pieces of clothes—T-shirts and shorts and other loose-fitting pieces—as possible.

For the first couple of months of school, this was fine. But the family lived in a northern state where it got really cold and snowy in the winter, so layers were a must. But Aiden couldn't put on multiple layers—that's how sensitive his skin was. When the cold weather hit, Aiden wasn't allowed to go out for recess, and he so badly wanted to play with his friends that he'd try his mightiest to force the layers on. But it was so painful that he'd start crying, which just confused his friends.

Aiden had to stay inside, and that made him feel left out. It also didn't help that Aiden struggled transitioning from one activity to the next. He didn't listen or pay attention to his teacher, and soon Bree and Clint were getting reports from Aiden's teacher about his struggles. The teacher suggested Aiden get tested. Clint and Bree felt paralyzed watching their son struggle physically, emotionally, and now academically and socially in school.

There were so many issues to sort out that Bree and Clint didn't know where to start. They felt helpless. And seeing your child suffering and not knowing how to fix it is the worst feeling as a parent.

MODERN CHALLENGES

Our society is only about 100 to 150 years away from having lived without electricity, refrigeration, telephones, and staying up all night watching movies and television. Through harnessing the elements, creating machines, and technology, we, humans, created a brave new world—one filled with more stressors, foods, products, and chemicals than our bodies have ever experienced.

But while our world has rapidly evolved, our bodies haven't.

Our kids are growing up and coming of age during a toxic time— perhaps the most toxic ever. From the air they breathe, to the toys they play with, to the foods they eat, to the skin care products they use, toxins hide in everything, bombarding their bodies in ways that we, our parents, and grandparents never experienced.

The more toxins our kids get exposed to, the more stress it places on their internal systems to detoxify. For many kids, the toxic load is too much for their bodies to handle.

Imagine you have a mason jar that represents your body. Inside the mason jar is water, and that represents toxins. Every day, we're exposed to toxins in our environments. In an ideal world, your body will eliminate toxins—it was designed to do this. But over time, we can be exposed to so many toxins that our body will not be able to keep pace with eliminating them.

Those toxins can disrupt our microbiome, causing imbalances in gut bacteria, which can affect our abilities to properly digest food and absorb nutrients and minerals, wreaking havoc on the endocrine system and hormones, which can adversely affect moods and behaviors. Even neurological development can get stunted and impaired.

Many kids today—and adults too—walk through the world with bodies riddled with inflammation. Jenny Carr, an inflammation expert, knows this all too well. She herself battled a severe toxic overload in her body that depleted her energy and strength and stole her ability to be present and engaged with her two children. As Jenny described, inflammation is essentially toxins in the body. Too much inflammation can cause skin conditions, stomach issues including constipation and diarrhea, headaches, behavior issues, increased aggression, and other health conditions that most Western doctors can't effectively treat or understand.[1]

It's tempting to want to put our kids in a bubble and eliminate all exposure, but that's impossible. We live in a toxic world, and the best we can do—the only thing we can do—is to try to limit our kids' exposure.

We can opt for healthier, more natural options that reduce our children's toxic exposure. And it comes down to prioritizing too. We can drive ourselves batty, possibly in debt, trying to find the perfect foods, household cleaners, and skin products. Realistically, you will need to get the biggest bang for your buck, within reason and budget.

Do your best to support your kids, while understanding and accepting the world as it is. We can commit and take real, practical steps to significantly reduce the toxins our kids get exposed to. You have more power than you may realize.

DIET AND NUTRITION:
A STRONG OR SHAKY FOUNDATION?

As humans, we need food to survive. Unfortunately, our food supply has massively changed in the last few decades. Pesticides and fertilizers are sprayed on our plants and fruits. Chemicals and additives are added to processed food. Antibiotics and hormones are injected into animals living under inhumane conditions. Is it any wonder that our kids' systems are out of whack?

Getting our kids to eat healthier foods is truly a game-changer for their health, development, and behavior. We're not reporting breaking news, and yet, let's get real, it's hard sometimes to feed our families healthy, wholesome foods. We're stretched for time and money, and sometimes we're just plain exhausted and don't have it in us to fight with our kids over what they're eating.

Still, we're learning just how harmful certain foods can be to our kids—and us. Increasingly, experts are talking about how food can cause inflammation in our bodies that affects everything from skin conditions to digestion to brain development, focus, and fogginess, to exhaustion to poor sleep to autoimmune diseases to being on the autism spectrum, to aggressive or bad behaviors.

Let's take a quick look at four of the most inflammatory foods:

Processed sugar. When it comes to our kids' foods, the sneakiest and most harmful ingredient isn't gluten or dairy, although those two get a ton of press. According to Jenny Carr, an inflammation expert, processed sugar takes the top spot. Most parents know they should avoid foods with high-fructose corn syrup or sugar cane, but processed sugar gets put into supposedly "healthy" foods like apple juice, deli meats, canned soups, and many store-bought breads. "I believe with all my heart that we are missing the ticket when we focus so much on removing gluten and cow's dairy," said Jenny.[2] "We have to take a stronger stance when it comes to processed sugar."[3]

Modernized wheat. All the rage right now is clean eating or going gluten-free. While that can certainly help, it may not be the silver bullet people think it is. If we're going to go gluten-free, then we need to make sure we're not substituting that with chemical-laden, highly inflammatory ingredients. That means we have to read the labels closely. Remember how in the 1990s, we thought taking out fat was the way to go? We saw fat-free products fill the shelves at the grocery store. But those products were loaded with a lot of sugar, which made people sick. We're repeating the same mistake with the gluten-free fad. It worked really well at the beginning of its introduction. People stopped eating bread and baked goods, and everything that had processed sugar and refined oils—all of which are inflammatory. But now the multibillion-dollar food industry has caught on, and they're labeling products "gluten-free" that are full of highly addictive toxins and chemicals. Just because a label says "gluten-free" doesn't mean that it's automatically healthier.

Dairy from cow's milk. Our bodies naturally produce digestive enzymes that help break down the foods we eat. Go way back to our hunter and gatherer ancestors, and typically, children would have nursed until the ages of three, maybe four years old. Our bodies adapted to create more digestive enzymes to break down the lactose found in our mother's breast milk. After age three or four, our bodies stop producing the same amounts of digestive enzymes needed to properly break down lactose. Cow's milk, which has played a huge role in most Western diets, also has a very large protein molecule. So when our bodies aren't producing as many digestive enzymes, it becomes harder for our children to properly digest and absorb the nutrients and minerals from milk, including cow's milk.

In addition, dairy from cows has changed quite significantly over the years, much like our other food. Today, many dairy farmers add antibiotics and hormones to their cows so they stay healthy and can produce more milk. Milk is also pasteurized. If you went back in time to how many of our grandparents got milk from the milkman, it was a daily delivery of fresh, minimally processed milk that had cream on top.

The third challenge comes from what dairy cows eat. That's corn, wheat, and soy—all inflammatory foods on their own, and they're the most genetically modified foods, which experts say are also inflammatory. Jenny Carr suspects that the food that cows eat plays a large role in causing inflammation: "Whether it's coming out as milk, cheese, or meat, we ingest all those things [antibiotics, hormones, corn, wheat, and soy], and they get passed on to us and we get inflamed."[4]

Hydrogenated oils. The list is long of what we don't want to use—refined vegetable oil, canola, corn, peanut, and seed-based oils. Seeds may sound strange, since we're told about their many health benefits. In their natural form, absolutely. But when seeds have been heated, they shift on a molecular level and can cause an inflammatory response.

When we remove these inflammatory foods from our kids' diets, it's like a new child appears. The same when many parents change their diets too. Julie Matthews, a registered dietician, often works with children on the autism spectrum with health conditions. While it's a very individualized diagnosis, many of these children struggle to properly digest gluten and dairy.

When Julie suggests to parents that they remove gluten and dairy from their kids' diets, she also recommends that the entire family adopt the same habits. Not only is it easier, but everyone tends to benefit. One mother whom Julie worked with lost 70 pounds by removing gluten and dairy.

We can significantly reduce the toxic load and inflammatory health responses in our kids just by dialing in to their diets and making adjustments. And while it takes planning, effort, and some time, the benefits go beyond their immediate health. These are healthy lifestyle practices our kids can carry with them forever.

Conscious Parenting Suggestion: Create a Healthier Diet

There's so much ground to cover when it comes to food and nutrition. We're tapping into some of the greatest hits in this section to help you turn the corner and get started.

Remove Inflammatory Foods by Making Healthier Swaps

Finding the "right" diet for our kids can feel confusing and overwhelming, especially now when we hear about different diets like keto, low-calorie, and Paleo, and next week, we're sure another one will be announced. As much as we all want to be handed the one-and-only diet to follow, it doesn't exist. There is no such thing as the perfect diet that works for everyone.

However, there are some solid nutritional principles that can help reduce inflammation in our kids. Just removing the most inflammatory foods (processed sugar, gluten, dairy from cow's milk, and hydrogenated oils) can make a huge difference.

When we say removing, we really mean substituting those inflammatory ingredients with healthier options. According to Jenny Carr, some of the best and easiest substitutions to make that will reduce inflammation and help our children's bodies to grow strong and healthy include the following:

Sub natural sugar or sweeteners for processed sugar. We have traditions and celebrations, and eating sweets is a part of our kids' culture and growing up. But processed sugar lurks in many of those sweet treats. Thankfully, we have substitutions that we can use, including unrefined coconut sugar, raw honey, pure maple syrup, and natural sugars and natural sweeteners such as monk fruit powder, liquid Stevia, and agave syrup.

Ditch wheat and go for alternative flours. When it comes to baking your kids' favorite treats, Jenny suggests nixing white and wheat flours and instead opting for almond, coconut, or cassava—or go wild and scour the shelves at your local health food store or in the organic or baking section of your local grocery store and experiment with chickpea, spelt, buckwheat, or other flours you find.

Opt for goat or sheep's milk products instead of dairy from cows. Many kids who struggle to break down cow's milk dairy can handle goat or sheep's milk products. Goat and sheep milks have much smaller protein molecules that make digesting them easier. Bonus: these options are typically higher in protein. Plus, goats and sheep aren't usually given corn or soy for their feed either, so you're reducing the inflammatory foods further. For most families, yogurt plays a key role in their kids' diets, so look for easy swaps here. There are many alternatives on the shelves today, such as coconut and cashew yogurt. And watch for the flavored yogurt. Although our kids likely enjoy it, it is often filled with additives and artificial sweeteners. A healthier choice is to go for plain and add your own sweetener like a little raw honey, pure maple syrup, or liquid Stevia.

Use coconut, avocado, and olive oils instead of vegetable or seed oils. Some of the best options you can turn to include unrefined cold-pressed coconut oil and avocado oil. You can use both at very high temperatures without them burning or going rancid. Extra-virgin olive oil is another great choice that gives amazing health benefits, although you have to use it at a lower temperature.

If you're feeling overwhelmed, we get it. Revamping our kids' diets and getting them onboard with healthier options is the bane of most parents' existence. So make one swap and then another. The best place to start? Processed sugar. Try nixing that from your kids' lives for two weeks. That's how little time it takes to push out inflammation and to start feeling results. Make it a family affair too.

None of us need processed sugar. If Mom and Dad nix their sugar fix, then they lead by example.

This doesn't have to be an all-or-nothing deal either. Aim to remove these ingredients most of the time—making them the exception. Now, if your kiddo suffers from a chronic illness, a behavioral or emotional issue, chronic anxiety, or a physical sensation that impacts their bodies or how they feel and can function day-to-day, their inflammatory signs might mean they are not be able to tolerate any bite.

Pay attention, watch for changes, and let them guide you.

Consider Adding More Pre- and Probiotics

Prebiotics found in vegetables, fruits, and legumes are filled with fiber, which the good bacteria in our stomachs love to eat. Probiotics are live bacteria—the good ones—found in fermented foods like pickles, sauerkraut, and kimchi. By introducing more pre- and probiotics into our kids' diets, we can help keep ear and yeast infections and other illnesses at bay by supporting the microbiome health. The healthier the microbiome, the less inflammation, the easier it is to detox, and the less susceptible to toxic overload our kids become.

Make Sure Kids Drink Plenty of Water

Drinking water is about more than hydration; it's about detoxing. Water helps flush out toxins and allows the liver and kidneys to function properly. We want to make sure our kids are drinking enough water (not the sugary fruit drinks or carbonated sodas) so they can eliminate toxins easier. Also, don't fall for the trick that water needs flavoring. Check the labels on those bottles, and you're bound to find words you can't pronounce. If your kid needs some flavoring, toss a lemon or cucumber slice into their glass.

Talk about How the Body Feels after Eating

In her home, Katie Kimball talks with her kids about how they feel after they eat. As an online kids' cooking teacher and a real-food blogger who helps families create healthy meals, Katie believes it's important to start the food-body connection going early. That's because many Americans live with a low level of pain that they've grown used to and think is normal. It's not. And a lot of that pain can come from inflammation caused by food choices. "As a society, we've never been taught to be mindful about how certain foods make us feel. Like if I eat bread and it makes me feel bloated or after I eat potatoes, I always feel foggy in my brain," said Katie.[5]

As Katie told us, we have an incredible opportunity to teach our kids about nutrition and health and the connection between food and their bodies before too much pain and damage set in. The more we talk about how we feel after eating certain foods and the more we help them to connect with how they feel, the more body awareness and consciousness we're helping them to create.

The cleaner the eating they do, the more they will notice how their bodies feel and the connection between food and their bodies. Ask your kids how they feel after they go to a friend's birthday party and have a piece of cake. Does their tummy hurt? Are they really tired? Do they have a pain in their stomach? Usually we have to describe how we feel first so they understand. Watch to see how they act. Do they start melting down or becoming more aggressive?

Find Your Child's Why

Everyone enjoys eating food. We all have cravings. Getting our kids to cut out processed sugar or white breads or sugary peanut butters can take some work. They may not want all the swaps, especially when their friends bring "the good stuff" to school for lunch.

One trick that Katie Kimball suggested was to find the connection between what our kids love to do and how eating healthier food will help them. For example, if your kid loves playing soccer, then try explaining how eating healthy fats and proteins gives them the energy to run up and down the soccer field. If they love singing, then explain how eating healthier foods will help their voice be strong and clear. If they love reading or school, share with them how healthier food will help them focus more and feel less distracted or tired.

Find out your kids' *why* by understanding how food can impact their lives—not how we see them, but how they're actually living them.

Get Your Kids in the Kitchen

When kids have a sense of ownership in the kitchen by making something or helping, they get excited about trying new foods. Bringing kids into the kitchen with you can make transitioning to healthier diets much easier.

Plus, it's another great way for us to connect with our kids. We're doing something together. We're creating something that's healthy and wholesome and that will feed and nourish our bodies and our souls. We're making something as a family unit that's challenging, but that our kids will take real pride in and want to eat.

Hide the Goods

Kids like sugars and sweets, fats, and all that unhealthy stuff because it tastes good. Vegetables and whole grains? Not so much. Don't be afraid to find ways to hide nutrients. Does your kid like smoothies? Throw in organic frozen spinach next time. They'll get the nutrients without insisting that they hate it.

WATCH YOUR EVERYDAY PRODUCTS

Every day our kids get exposed to thousands of chemicals and toxins, and while we'll never cut their exposure to zero, we can control and greatly reduce that number. That begins by becoming conscious about what daily products our kids use or are around. Let's dig into some of the most common ones that, when tweaked, can significantly reduce the toxic load in your kids. We're giving a general overview first, and then we'll offer some swaps in the suggestions section.

Diapers. We all love diapers for their super absorbency. However, many conventional brands use chemicals and tiny crystals to soak up the urine. These chemicals can cause skin issues and get into babies and toddlers' systems, disrupting their microbiomes, immune systems, and endocrine systems.

Cleaning supplies. Watch your kids, especially the young ones, as they move around the house, and what will you see? Tiny handprints everywhere. Them touching and crawling and grabbing everything. Those hands often go straight into their mouths too.

How often do you catch your kid dropping a small bowl of cereal or crackers on the coffee table or floor, only to snatch the food back up and pop it into their mouths? Probably a lot. This is what being a kid is. But if they're touching and moving across all of these surfaces and jamming their fingers into their mouths, then that also means they're picking up, ingesting, and absorbing whatever chemical residue has been left over from the cleaning supplies you used. We're not talking huge amounts, but it's little amounts that get into their system that build up over time or trigger sensitivity that can become problematic. It's the same idea when we use strong cleaners like bleach that give off intense odors. This can cause irritation in the respiratory system.

Furniture and bedding. Since the 1970s, flame retardants have been used in loads of products, from furniture to electronics to clothing, and it's to prevent them from going up in flames. That's a good thing. Except that chemicals can leak from these products into the air and water and can disrupt the immune system, the endocrine and thyroid systems, and can have adverse effects on fetal and childhood neurological development.[6]

Lunch boxes and food storage. Plastic wrap and baggies have become a staple in many kitchens for ease and convenience. While many companies use safer BPA-free plastic, it can take some digging to make sure the plastic is truly safe. There is also the danger of leaching, where the chemicals leak from the plastic into the food.

Air. The more polluted the air, the more our children can suffer from respiratory illnesses and infections. When we think of air pollution, we think of the great outdoors and certain locations like Los Angeles. It may surprise you to learn that studies are finding that indoor air quality may be more polluted than the great outdoors.[7] According to the EPA, most people spend as much as 90 percent of their time indoors, and the ones exposed to indoor air pollutants for the longest periods of time are often the most susceptible to its effects—one of those groups being the young.[8]

Water. In the United States, most people expect to turn on their kitchen faucet and voila, clean drinking water magically pours forth. That's true—sort of. Water treatment plants use chemicals like chlorine to disinfect the water and keep bad bacteria and dangerous diseases at bay. But tap water isn't as clean as we like to believe. For some people, chlorine and other disinfectants can impact their gut bacteria and cause adverse reactions. Some water can contain pharmaceuticals that get flushed down the toilet through urine or unused medications. Pesticides from farming, lead from old pipes, and even radioactive material from energy plants or defense weapons can leak into the water supply.

Skin care. "When you put something on your body, it takes only twenty-six seconds for it to be absorbed into your bloodstream, and it's really important for moms and families to understand that because there are so many things in skin care that can cause problems for hormones and the hormonal system, it can cause cancer and neurological problems," explained Trina Felber, a registered nurse with a master's degree in nursing and the CEO of Primal Life Organics, a company specializing in plant-based, nutritional skin care and dental products.[9] Think about what your kids use, from sunscreens to lotions to deodorants. Unlike food, which first goes through a digestive process, skin care products and all the chemicals in them get absorbed directly into our kids' bloodstream. There is no line of defense, so toxins get carried throughout and can settle anywhere in their bodies—fatty tissue, muscle, the brain.

Conscious Parenting Suggestion:
When Possible, Go Natural

We're running down a list of possible alternatives to get you out of the gate. When in doubt? Aim for natural, organic products. "I like to have as many things that will touch my child's skin or go into their body to be as natural as possible," explained Julie Matthews, a certified nutrition consultant and educator.[10] "It's not always the case, but that's my rule of thumb."[11]

Keep in mind, you don't need to break the bank or address all of these at once. Try focusing on one area and make gradual changes that are practical and doable.

Choose organic diapers. According to Dr. Christian Gonzalez, a naturopathic doctor, we want to look for organic diapers that use organic cotton and that minimize the amount of absorbency area. These diapers also contain different materials, which tend to be safer for our youngest family members.[12]

Go for all-natural cleaners. Look for nontoxic and environmentally safe cleaners. You can also look for "Safer Choice" labels that meet the U.S. EPA Safer Product Standards.

Go for green furniture. If you want to switch your furniture, it can be done. It can take time to find the right companies and it may cost more, but you can decorate your home with furniture made from water-based glues and organic fabrics for couches, chairs, and mattresses.

Opt for safer materials for lunch containers and food storage materials. We have more options than plastic and plastic baggies for our kids' lunches. Now we can use silicone or stainless steel or glass containers. All are reusable, so not only can we cut down on toxicity, we can also save money. That's a win-win.

Get an air filter. If you want to ensure the air quality in your home stays clean, consider buying an air filter that can remove particulates, pollen, and mold from the air. You can buy whole-house filters that can cover thousands of square feet, portable air filters that cover hundreds of square feet, or a filter for your furnace. Look for units that have HEPA filters—that's the gold standard that removes the most pathogens. Depending on where you live, opening windows to allow in more fresh air and better ventilation is also a solution.

Use a water filter. Just like air filtration systems, you can buy water ones too. These can hook to your kitchen faucet and filter out most chemicals and toxins, including prescription drug residue and chlorine, from your drinking water.

Choose healthy skin care products. With so many products on shelves today, it's easy to feel overwhelmed by choices and unsure what products to trust. Trina Felber, a registered nurse and CEO of Primal Life Organics, says it's all about label reading. "You can look at the ingredients and know within 5 to 10 seconds whether it's worth your health or your money."[13] Fortunately for us, Trina shared some of her top tips on what we should look for, including:

- **All plant-based ingredients.** Our bodies get nourished in two ways: through what we eat and what we put on our skin. Plant-based ingredients tend to be gentler, less irritating, and chemical-free, making these healthier choices for our kids.

- **No water, unless the label says "purified."** When water is the first ingredient, it usually makes up about 70–90 percent of the product. Unless a skin care company says the water is purified, then we're likely using a product that can contain different toxins commonly found in everyday tap water, including heavy metals, radioactive material, or drug waste. Water also disrupts the protective layer of oil on our skin by pulling out moisture, which can affect our microbiome, creating an imbalance between our good and bad bacteria.

- **No fragrances.** When a company wants a product to smell good, they can go to a database and pick from different chemicals that, when combined, make that scent. But the company doesn't have to reveal what they used to make that scent, because it's considered a trade secret. As Trina explained, that database is often filled with toxins, and most products that make up fragrance can cause cancers, health problems, issues with the endocrine (hormone) system, or neurological issues. They can also cause allergies and skin conditions.

- **No "unscented" label.** It's an easy mistake to make. We grab the "unscented" product believing that we're avoiding harmful fragrances. Unfortunately that doesn't mean our kids get exposed to fewer toxins; "unscented" often means the toxins are getting covered up with a neutralizing scent.

TOXINS AND THE CONNECTION TO AUTISM AND SPECIAL NEEDS

We cannot leave the toxins discussion without addressing the autism spectrum and children with special needs. It's one of the biggest health challenges facing millions of children and their families today and it's growing every year. In 2000, about 1 in 150 children were diagnosed on the autism spectrum. By 2010, that number climbed to 1 in 68,[14] and by 2016, it was 1 in 54.[15] Children in New Jersey report the highest percentages with 1 in 32.[16]

What is going on in our lives or our environment that could be responsible for making the statistics go in such a shocking direction? Dr. Darin Ingels, a naturopathic physician specializing in autism and chronic immune problems, shared that research has heavily focused on genetics as the culprit, but he remains unconvinced. "There's been speculation that there is a genetic aspect of autism, but there's no such thing as a genetic epidemic. Genetics alone do not explain the fact that we have seen autism move at this epidemic rate."[17]

Dr. Ingels has treated thousands of children from infants to young adults in their twenties. He believes the best explanation for the autism spectrum lies in toxins our children get exposed to, starting as early as when their mothers conceived. "We don't really know what causes autism to develop for every child, but there's a good speculation that a lot of it comes back to what's going on in the environment. Our kids are getting bombarded with so many different toxins between what they eat and what they breathe that affect their neurodevelopment," Dr. Ingels said.[18]

Autism is a complex health condition that manifests differently in each child. It can include developmental delays that affect language, speech, motor, brain, or physical activity. Many children can struggle to communicate with their families, eat, and function in their day-to-day lives. Children with autism also often have multiple health conditions that can impact their gut, kidneys, senses, and brain and neurological functioning.

The medical community has made huge strides in the last couple of decades in treating kids diagnosed with autism and other special needs. Dr. Ingels has discovered that when he starts addressing medical problems one at a time, children improve. He sees their language, behavior, sleep, bowel movements, and digestion get better. "It's about getting to the root of these underlying medical issues that are potential triggers for autism, and as we get the body to heal, we see these kids improve," he explained.[19]

This was Billy's story. Dr. Ingels began seeing Billy when he was three years old. As Billy's mother described, when Billy was born, he was a colicky baby who had a hard time breastfeeding. She started him on formula, but he would throw it up, have loose stools or diarrhea, and would get a bloated, distended abdomen. This went on for many months, and when Billy's mom brought him to the pediatrician, the doctor said it was normal and everything was fine. Around age two, Billy's mom grew concerned. Billy wasn't speaking. He had no language at all, but again, the pediatrician told her it was fine and that boys talk later than girls.

By the time Dr. Ingels saw Billy, he still had no language, when he should have had at least a couple hundred words. He had terrible bowel movements and suffered from a lot of stomach pain. Nothing about Billy's development had been normal, despite what Billy's pediatrician said.

"We're seeing not only an epidemic of autism, but an epidemic of doctors failing to recognize these early signs so that we can start earlier intervention," said Dr. Ingels.[20]

Dr. Ingels sees thousands of kids just like Billy every year, and while the health conditions vary from child to child, most share one common factor. "Across the board in kids with autism, they don't detox well," shared Dr. Ingels.[21] "When they get exposed to different toxins, their ability to get rid of them may not be as good as other children. So we have to go backward and start working on therapies that are specifically designed to help improve their ability to detoxify."[22]

That includes making sure the child has the right gut bacteria and then working to address their unique health conditions, whether that's dealing with headaches or a spine or posture that needs correcting. Dr. Ingels typically works with physical, speech, or occupational therapists.

Addressing autism is a very collaborative effort—that's how complex it is.

There is no one treatment, let alone a pill, that will work; it's step by step, giving kids time and monitoring to see how they improve. But improvement can happen. "If we start focusing more on healing them from the inside out, then we see their behavior, cognition, and language improve," explained Dr. Ingels.[23]

As Dr. Ingels shared, he has seen kids in his practice recover, meaning they go back to their pediatrician and the children no longer receive a diagnosis of being on the spectrum.

The earlier the treatment can happen, the better the odds of a child reaching recovery. Recovery truly may be possible, but it takes work, time, patience. While it's better to catch this when a child is young, it's never too late. Dr. Ingels had a patient come to him who was 21 years old and nonverbal. He had about three or four words. After working with him for two years, Dr. Ingels's patient is now conversational and has a job. "The brain has the ability to change and be flexible," said Dr. Ingels. "It's just a function of finding the right interventions for the right person."[24]

If you take nothing else away from this section, please take hope. There are paths through the maze that is raising a child on the spectrum. It will take time and patience, but it can be achieved by connecting different treatments and working with doctors who truly understand this health condition.

Conscious Parenting Suggestion:
Work with Autism and Special Needs Experts

It's devastating for a family to learn their child is on the spectrum.

While many families get caught up in denial—refusing to acknowledge or accept their child has special needs—the earlier they can take action, the better chances a child has to recover. The best suggestion our experts all shared was to please seek help and expertise from a practitioner who specializes in treating special needs children. "Find practitioners who have a deep understanding of autism, who are going to be willing to work with you on diet, nutrition, sleep, and all these other aspects of improving their [your child's] health," said Dr. Ingels.[25]

"As you get their health improved, you will see your child improve. If you do nothing, you will get nothing. And if you do something, you will get something. And most of the kids we work with, we do see some level of improvement," explained Dr. Ingels.[26]

Try looking in your area or in the nearest large urban area for a doctor who treats special needs children. This may require working with a naturopath, integrative, or functional medical practitioner rather than a standard Western-trained pediatrician.

You may want to look for an expert certified by MAPS (Medical Academy of Pediatric Special Needs), and there is also a group called TACA (The Autism Community in Action, tacanow.org) that has many resources and information that can help you on this quest.

We already talked a lot about the role diet plays in inflammation, so we won't hit this too hard here. But it's worth mentioning that diet and nutrition typically play a big role in helping reverse autism and special needs diagnoses. Julie Matthews, a certified nutrition consultant and educator, explained to us, most special needs children cannot properly digest gluten and dairy, so when those foods get removed from their diets, kids' bodies start healing, which has positive ripples throughout their lives.

Julie co-authored the study "Comprehensive Nutritional and Dietary Intervention for Autism Spectrum Disorder—A Randomized, Controlled 12-Month Trial," published in the scientific journal *Nutrients*,[27] which found that a healthy gluten-free, casein-free (casein is found in dairy), and soy-free diet, along with nutrients such as a multivitamin/mineral formula and essential fatty acids, decrease digestive symptoms; improve developmental age by 4.5 times over; increase IQ points by 6.7; reduce anxiety, depression, and aggression; and improve cognitive thinking, attention/focus, and sociability.[28]

Diet plays a huge role, but as Julie cautioned, it's a journey, not a destination. Like most treatments, it takes time. Keep "nourishing hope," as Julie says.[29] That combined with finding the right experts and never giving up can help you change the trajectory and quality of your child's life.

BECOMING CONSCIOUS

Bree and Clint coasted for a few years before Bree discovered an anti-inflammatory health coach. It was Bree's own health conditions that initially led her down this road. She had become so stressed with Aiden's health conditions that her system got shot. She felt bloated all the time and had such extreme exhaustion that she wanted to go to bed at five o'clock most days. She was constantly nauseous, depressed, and her hormones were out of whack. No doctor could figure it out. All they did know was that Bree was having some sort of autoimmune response.

Bree was willing to try anything, so when she found an anti-inflammation coach, she thought, *Let's just give it a shot.*

Thus she began swapping inflammatory foods, starting with removing processed sugar from her diet, then gluten, then dairy. Within a few months, Bree felt like a new person! Her health conditions had cleared up so much that she thought that if an anti-inflammatory diet had helped her, then maybe it could help Aiden too.

She and Clint decided to have the whole family try this new, anti-inflammatory diet. Bree and Clint committed to completely changing breakfast, lunch, dinner, desserts, and snacks. In a two-week experiment, they removed the top inflammatory foods, including processed sugars, gluten, dairy, and hydrogenated oils.

They were astounded by the results. Within two weeks, Aiden had significantly improved. His sensory issues had diminished, and he could wear more layers of clothing. Aiden's focus and concentration and ability to calmly transition from activities improved too. It was like they had a new little boy.

Clint felt better too. He had lost 11 pounds, and he felt lighter and happier, had more energy, and clearer sinuses. He had never noticed how stuffy his nose and sinuses had felt before.

Bree and Clint knew they had to maintain this new way of eating and began their transition to maintaining an anti-inflammatory diet. They both agreed that they had to find ways for it not to feel overwhelming or that they were depriving themselves or Aiden of tasty food.

One thing that has helped Bree get Aiden excited about these food changes was talking to him about recess. Bree talked to Aiden about their new way of eating by explaining, "These healthy foods let you play outside at recess with your friends." She knew it was something he desperately wanted, so she tapped into his *why* to help him embrace the changes.

Changing her family's diet also inspired Bree to research and better understand the body's chemistry, microbiome, good versus bad bacteria, and connection between inflammation and toxins and chemicals. What she learned was that Aiden's sensory issues may have been caused by the extreme amount of antibiotics that had been pumped into his body to fight the infections. And while she may never find the one cause for Aiden's health challenges, she does believe that her son was born more sensitive to the world around him, where chemicals and toxins sometimes overwhelm his body's ability to detox itself, making him more prone to inflammation.

Bree has changed many of her family's household goods and cleaners too. She tries to stay away from plastic water bottles, and if she can't, she tries to keep them out of the sun to prevent chemicals from the plastic from leaking into the water. She doesn't microwave plastic even if it says it's safe. Everyone in her family has a stainless steel water canteen, and her kids use glass with rubber on the outside to bring their lunches to school. Bree also opts for organic vegetables and fruits, and free-range, hormone-free, and antibiotic-free meat. And she uses natural, green household cleaners, in addition to water purifiers for her kitchen faucet and a portable air filter.

Bree and Clint made these changes over the course of about three years. Each has taken an investment of their time and money, but they wholeheartedly believe it's been worth it. Aiden's chronic infections have dramatically dropped to just a couple of illnesses every year, but none that have required hospital stays or massive antibiotic treatments. His behavior has improved and he's a happy kid.

Aiden's body does remain pretty sensitive. When he goes to a friend's birthday party and eats a piece of cake, his body has a strong reaction. He gets bloated and he "melts down." Bree and Clint use these moments as teaching lessons for Aiden for talking to him about how his body feels after eating cake, so he understands the connection between what he eats and how he feels. And while it may taste good in the moment, it feels terrible later.

Overall, while it takes work and planning, Bree and Clint read the labels on canned or packaged food from the grocery store, both remaining committed to keeping inflammatory foods out of their diets and Aiden's.

Conscious Parenting Challenge

This is a two-week challenge: take out processed sugar from your family's diet. Look for healthy substitutes for everyone during this period and keep a journal. Notice how you feel and watch your kids' behavior. Do they change? Notice how they interact with you, their siblings, and your spouse/partner. Do they pay attention more? Do they listen? What about weight? If your kids are old enough, ask them about how they feel. Do their stomachs feel better? Do their heads feel clearer? Use words to describe how you're physically and emotionally feeling to prompt them. If you have to wrangle your spouse/partner to agree to this, then do it. Talk to them about why you want to try this and explain that it's just a little experiment to see how everyone in the family feels. And have fun!

(CHAPTER 8)

NATURE

Jim and Lesley were worried.

Their sons, Micah, 11, and Noah, 9, seemed to constantly fight. They knew some of this was typical for siblings. But at night, after the boys had gone to sleep, Jim and Lesley would agree that they were more concerned that Micah was at the root of the boys fighting.

Micah had always been serious. He cared a lot about his grades, which they had thought was a good thing. But if he got a B on a test or homework assignment, he would melt down at home. He would have angry, unexpected outbursts and seemed easily irritated. He directed a lot of that energy at Noah.

Jim thought Micah needed more physical outlets, but Micah hated organized sports. He had tried soccer, basketball, and lacrosse, but he lacked the hand-eye coordination needed to keep up with his peers.

Living in an urban environment made it difficult for Micah and Noah to get the physical activity that Jim sensed his sons, especially his oldest, needed. Lesley had been born and raised in a city and couldn't relate to Jim's point of view. Growing up in the Pacific Northwest, Jim had spent his childhood and all his free time traipsing through forests, fishing, and camping, and just playing outside until it got so dark that he had to go home. These were some of his fondest memories of growing up.

Jim often felt guilty that his sons were growing up surrounded by concrete instead of nature, but his and Lesley's corporate jobs kept them tied to urban life. Deep down, Jim felt that Micah—and

Noah—would benefit from more time running and playing in nature. Something inside of Jim told him that if Micah could be outside more, then maybe he wouldn't be so angry or irritable all the time.

When he voiced this to Lesley, she agreed that the kids needed more exercise and to spend time outside, but how, when, and where?

They had a small patch of land in the back that could hardly be considered a yard, and the nearest park or open space was at least a 20-minute walk from their home. Both Lesley and Jim worked full-time, and they didn't want the kids going to the park alone without them.

If Jim wanted his boys to spend more time outside, then it was going to take more effort on his part to find a way to make that happen.

MODERN CHALLENGES

When you think back on your childhood, what are some of your favorite memories?

For us, it was riding our bikes with our friends, shooting hoops at our neighborhood courts, going to the beach, and trekking through the woods. Getting dirty, sweating, and being outdoors was all we wanted to do.

We weren't unique for kids growing up in the 1970s and 1980s.

But times have changed, and what once was a quintessential rite of childhood is becoming obsolete. Kids growing up today are spending less time outside than ever before. There are real reasons for this. We can point to technology and all the devices that vie for our kids' attention. There are the hours of homework they get assigned, and extracurricular activities keep their schedules full and spare time limited.

And sometimes there just aren't the green spaces or safe places for them to play outside. Many kids growing up in urban environments can't just walk out their back door and have acres of open space or woodlands to explore.

We can tick off all the reasons why our kids aren't getting outdoors. We can rationalize them too, and sometimes there are real barriers. Still, there's a toll, and our kids are paying for this emotionally, mentally, physically, and spiritually. We are a part of nature, and while we may have migrated to live the majority of our lives inside, a part of us still yearns for where we came from.

Connecting to the sun, wind, stars, moon, trees, and animals and finding our place within the cosmic web is our birthright. Our society may have forgotten this, but it's impossible to see ourselves as separate. We can no more defy the laws of gravity than we can deny our place as part of Mother Nature. So has it always been, and so will it always be.

Fortunately, we have the power to do something about this. We can reverse the trend and get our kids—and ourselves—outdoors, connecting to Mother Nature.

We have to admit, of all the suggestions that we make, perhaps none are more fun than the ones for bringing nature back into our children's—and our families'—lives. We hope that you see and feel this too. Spending time outside in nature with family creates lifelong memories and unbreakable bonds that everyone will cherish and remember.

For those families living in urban areas, we know that it can take more planning and creativity to incorporate nature into your child's life. Regardless of where you live, this is your chance to try new adventures outdoors, visit new and wondrous places, and expose your kids to something different. It may take a few tries to find the right activities that your family enjoys as a group. If that happens, don't worry. Stick with it. As long as you make being outside a priority, you'll eventually find the right ways for everyone to connect with the great outdoors.

Go and have fun. Let your child return to their birthright, reconnect with Mother Nature, and restore their place in the Universe of all things.

BOOSTING HEALTH AND WELLNESS

In the United States, we have a mental health crisis affecting our children.

If that sounds alarmist, it's meant to. The Centers for Disease Control and Prevention reports that 1 in 5 American children between the ages of 3 and 17—about 15 million—have a diagnosable mental, emotional, or behavioral disorder in a given year,[1] but only 20 percent of those kids receive any treatment.[2]

This is as heartbreaking as it is dangerous. Our kids are unwell, and it's on us to figure this out.

Kids today face extraordinary pressures—many that we've already chronicled, including stress from school, too much technology, consumerism on steroids, and too many toxins in their food and environment.

And we can add another to that list: the loss of nature.

Richard Louv, a journalist and author of *Last Child in the Woods*, coined the term *nature deficit disorder*. "That was a tongue-in-cheek phrase when I used it," Richard told us.[3] "It caught on and entered the language—several languages—because it gave parents and teachers a way to talk about what we knew was going on. We felt it. We had no name for it, which was that our children were not getting outside very much, and I'm not talking about playing soccer. They were not engaging in the natural world like other generations did and that they had taken for granted."[4]

As Richard continued, "There are psychological costs, spiritual costs, there are also social, even democratic costs to not being outside. In order to have a democracy, people have to go outdoors and meet their neighbors. To have any kind of intelligent view about the natural world, about the world itself, you have to engage in nature."[5]

There are also health consequences for our kids spending so much time indoors. For all the modern conveniences of electricity and the technological revolution that we've enjoyed for the last 200 years, it has some measurable downsides. For one, it has disrupted our *circadian rhythm*. This is the natural sleep-wake cycle that tells our bodies when it's time to wake up and be active versus to power down, fall asleep, and heal from the day's activities.

Sunlight powers our circadian rhythm. During the day, the sun gives off a blue light wavelength that tells our bodies we need to be awake. When the sun sets, it gives off a red-light wavelength that triggers the hormone melatonin, which helps our bodies fall and stay asleep.

The electronic devices that our kids use right up until they go to sleep give off blue light wavelengths that signal to their bodies that they need to stay awake. The less time our kids spend outdoors and the more that they're in front of a screen, the harder it becomes for them to fall and stay asleep. Lack of sleep creates cascading problems that can lead to anxiety and depression.

Living life indoors and under fluorescent light also means our kids catch fewer rays from the sun. That means they're not soaking up vitamin D. Low levels of vitamin D can lead to immune system issues that can cause asthma, eczema, and allergies, and it can also lead to greater anxiety and depression.

The good news is that just getting our kids outside in Mother Nature rejuvenates and restores them. For instance, anxiety is a fear of the future and what could be. It can leave kids feeling ungrounded and untethered to the present. Just being outside can help alleviate that anxiety by taking kids out of their heads and putting them in their bodies. Talk to an occupational therapist. When they're teaching children stability with walking, an occupational therapist may recommend not wearing any shoes and walking barefoot on the grass. That's because the ground feels more solid and kids feel that. The more solid they feel, the more stable they will become. That's as emotionally and mentally true as it is physically.

We're also seeing more pediatricians recognize the need for nature in their young patients' lives. Richard shared with us his experience giving a keynote speech to members of the American Academy of Pediatrics. "Nature deficit disorder is not a known medical diagnosis; maybe it should be, but it's not. I was surprised to be asked, and nervous because it was a very important group. If there was anybody that could affect children more than teachers, in terms of the future relationship between children and the natural world, it was pediatricians, who are trusted by parents."[6]

The speech seemed to be well received by the audience. Doctors said they were going to return to their practices and start writing prescriptions. "I was stunned by their reactions and by hearing them say they would change their practices, but I thought, I'm not going to hold my breath. But then, many of them did."[7]

One of those doctors was Dr. Robert Zarr, a pediatrician who practiced in Washington, D.C. When Dr. Zarr returned to his practice after the conference, he began writing "nature prescriptions" to his patients. He showed parents where the closest park to their home was and gave them suggestions on what to do with their kids. Dr. Zarr didn't stop there. He went on to organize other pediatricians in the D.C. area, and he created a database of all the parks and open spaces in their community so doctors could quickly turn to the computer, find the nearest park, and write nature prescriptions for their patients too.

Dr. Zarr went on to become the founder and medical director of Park Rx America, a community health initiative that prescribes nature to patients and families to prevent and treat chronic disease and promote wellness.[8] "Over 400 correlational studies have thus far shown improved health outcomes directly related to time spent in nature," wrote Dr. Zarr. "It is rare for doctors to find such an accessible and inexpensive intervention that positively impacts a wide breadth of chronic disease, ranging from diabetes to high blood pressure to obesity to depression and many other serious mental illnesses, found in all ages."[9]

Like many of the issues that we have discussed, we know that pivoting from the typical routine can be tough. Our lives have largely evolved to bring us indoors, so it takes concerted effort, planning, and intention to return to nature and to get our kids out there. Still, the benefits for our kids, ourselves, and our families are so numerous that we owe it to everyone to make this a priority.

Conscious Parenting Suggestion: Get Kids Outdoors

Now that we're all onboard with getting kids outdoors more, how can we make that happen? The most important way is to keep it simple. Go for easy and fun, and remember that something is better than nothing. Plus, it doesn't take that much time for our kids to reap the health benefits.

A recent study found that people only need to spend two hours in nature per week in natural spaces such as parks, beaches, and woodlands.[10] It didn't even matter if those 120 minutes were recorded all at once or over the week.[11]

Two hours. That's attainable. Think about how quickly two hours goes by when your kids play video games or binge a show. Just cut back on their technology time, get them outside, and you may find out that they prefer trees to their devices.

Be the Example

It always comes back to us. We set the example for our children's behavior, so if we want them to be outside, we have to do it first. Of course, there is no harm in telling our kids to go play outside by themselves.

Still, as conscious parents, we have a responsibility to create opportunities for our kids to be outdoors connecting with nature. And like most things in life, we have to show them how. We have to introduce them to nature, whether that's taking them hiking, biking, camping, swimming, skiing, snowshoeing, climbing trees, to the park, or just lying on the ground with them.

What we do outside with them is less important than just getting outside together.

Go with your interests, try new activities, see what your kids gravitate to. We don't have to know every tree, plant, or animal. In fact, it's better that we don't. "Don't pretend to know everything and don't feel guilty that you don't," said Richard. "Let your kid find out the names of the animal or plant, or ignore it and just watch it, get to know it, and have that sense of wonder. The important thing is for your kid to see you have that sense of wonder and surprise and awe. That communicates far more than any book and far more than any name for that animal."[12]

Besides just getting your kids outdoors, try picking an activity that the family can learn together. There are a lot of clubs that welcome beginners, so take advantage of those or take lessons—if that's in the budget. Be creative and make it fun for the whole family.

Breathing the fresh air, soaking up the sun's rays, and basking in the natural world reduces our stress, helps relieve us from burnout and exhaustion, and restores and renews our connection to the world.

As guys who love spending time outdoors hiking and skiing—two of our favorite passions—and sharing the wonders with our kids and as a family too, it is the ultimate win-win for everyone. Guaranteed.

Lie on the Ground and Look Up

The next time your kids seem wired, stop what you're doing and take them outside. Find a nice spot on the lawn, or at a park or beach, lie on the ground, and stare up at the sky. This can be during the day or at night. Do this with them. Lie next to them and don't talk.

Focus on taking big, deep belly breaths, breathing in through the nose, and filling the abdomen. Have them hold each breath for a few seconds, and then slowly exhale. Do this about five or seven times, or as many as needed.

When it feels right, talk to your kids about what they see in the sky. Ask them what pictures they see and what the clouds look like. Ask them about the stars. This is the ultimate grounding technique that can help them calm their nervous systems and minds.

It sounds simple, because it is. And yet, it's like magic. It's one of the most basic exercises, and it only costs time to do. No training or fancy equipment. Anyone, anywhere can do this.

Check Out Ecopsychology

If your child is struggling with anxiety or another mental health issue, and you want to see a therapist, consider working with someone who uses ecopsychology. It's a practice that has emerged in the last few decades, where therapists bring nature into their practices.

Some therapists will hold sessions outdoors, or they may bring animals into the practice. Animals are incredible for helping kids reconnect to nature and to something fundamental within themselves. Animals are grounding too.

Summer Lall, a music therapist, heavily features nature in her work with middle to high school students, including some gang members, in Los Angeles. Many of her patients live in an urban jungle, never seeing or having much exposure to green space. Summer believes reconnection to nature can be powerful medicine for them. Sometimes during their sessions, she will bring them into her garden, where numerous elements from nature wait for them.

Summer's patients will practice mindfulness walking as Summer uses a buffalo drum to help keep their pace. She's set up an altar where kids can write the names of their deceased loved ones and friends on rocks that they place at the altar. She also keeps stones around that kids can hold to help ground them. Summer will sometimes weave in the sound of waves crashing or birds chirping because it helps the kids relax and focus.

Summer uses nature as a tool to evoke deep healing partly because she sees our innate connection to Mother Earth. "I don't consider that we live on nature," explained Summer.[13] "I think we *are* nature. We are part of the plant, part of this whole system that is incredible and intelligent beyond what we understand."

As Summer shared with us, humans have created roads and buildings on nature and the communities and lives that we have built have created separation between humankind and the natural world. This divorce has caused a lot of problems. "There's been a nature deficit with kids, and now there needs to be a reunification," Summer said.[14]

The way Summer explains her concept of nature can really shift our views. The natural world holds so much for our kids, especially for their healing.

CREATIVITY, CURIOSITY, AND IMAGINATION

Kids today are coming of age in a highly curated, overly produced world where images get projected out to them. With games and apps, kids punch in their passwords and boom! They're in the game that someone has created. Often they see entire worlds that are built for them.

It's the same idea with movies and shows they watch. One of the greatest benefits to reading or listening to a story is that kids use their imaginations to create images in their mind's eye. They create parts of the worlds and the stories. Because of this, Dr. Ana-Maria Temple, a functional medicine pediatrician says, "Our kids face death of creativity."[15]

There is perhaps no better place or way for our kids to develop their imaginations and creativity than in nature, which stimulates their minds in ways that no simulated play on a device can.

When we talk about a childlike sense of wonder and awe, we're talking about curiosity. Kids are born into this world curious. They want to know why. *If I do this, then what happens?* This is how they develop and understand the world around them. Life, for them, is cause and effect.

This curiosity—which supports their imaginations and creativity—will either be nurtured or is unintentionally snuffed out. No parent sets out to kill their kids' curiosity, imagination, or creativity. It's an unfortunate by-product of living in our modern world.

Thankfully, getting our kids outside in nature is an antidote. When kids spend time outside, they're naturally asking all kinds of questions. They're tapping into their senses—sound, smell, touch, sight, and sometimes taste.

What is this leaf? Why is it here? What is this rock? How did it get here? That's a big branch. Can I break it? Why did the water flow over the bank? What animal made these tracks in the mud? What bug is this? What happens if I snap this twig or pull off a piece of bark?

The natural scientist within them awakens, and they want to learn and understand the world around them. And nature, of course, lies at the root of science.

Physics, biology, chemistry, astronomy—all of these disciplines were born because people were curious. They wanted answers to: Why? How? What does this mean?

"Kids still have the ability to be imaginative, even with their electronics, but their creativity gets exponentially improved being outdoors," said Dr. Tiana Mondaca, a clinical psychologist.[16] "Spending time and playing in nature and being out back enhance their creativity and imagination."[17]

If we want our kids to flex and build their curiosity, imagination, and creativity muscles, then we have to get them outdoors, and sometimes that means by themselves. This thought terrifies some parents.

"It seems like parents are more afraid, like they feel the world is unsafe, which if you look statistically, it's not true," said Robin Ray Green, a licensed acupuncturist, pediatric acupuncture expert, and mother.[18] "But because we're so connected and there's so much information being shown to us, we feel it's possible for our child to be hurt, injured, or kidnapped. If you look statistically, that's not true, but we don't want to be that one mom who says, 'I let my kid go to the park by themselves and then they get kidnapped or something happens to them.' So we end up following them there, making sure they're okay," said Robin.[19]

"As parents, we're so absorbed in making sure they're safe, that I think we're overcompensating and not letting them explore," said Reena B. Patel, a child and educational psychologist specializing in behavior.[20] "Remember doing that when you were younger? Let them ride a bike. Maybe they'll fall, but they're going to get right back up. We have to let go a little bit and let them explore. Let's see how they navigate, and let's teach them resiliency."[21]

We're not advocating for a kids-gone-wild situation with an "anything-goes, who cares attitude." Living situations are unique, plus kids need different supervision depending on their ages. Do what is right for your situation and family.

Playing outdoors and being outside allows kids to take risks, learn from mistakes, and become more independent, all of which helps to keep them safer and make better choices in their lives as they grow up. This will not only stimulate their creativity and curiosity and imagination, it will teach them invaluable lessons in confidence, independence, and resiliency.

As we stated earlier, we are not anti-technology. This is the world that our kids are growing up in and which they will inherit. Understanding how to use these devices is a must. And our kids need balance too, and Mother Nature offers them it.

She gives and teaches, and can help us shape well-rounded, openhearted, and open-minded kids who will discover, create, and build the future.

Conscious Parenting Suggestion: Encourage the Connection

Getting our kids outdoors requires consciousness and action. How do we find the time? We make it.

Put It on the Calendar

"We should not assume that just because we have a backyard with some trees in it that our kids going outside will happen naturally," explained Richard Louv.[22] As he shared, we have to make the time and schedule it on the calendar, just like we would a soccer practice or any extracurricular activity.

Let Boredom Be the Guide

Dr. Tiana Mondaca told us an all-too-familiar story about how her son had a very difficult time being imaginative and playing outdoors. She'd tell him to go outside and play, and he'd respond with, "I don't know what to do. What do I do?" Sound familiar? We've been in those situations with our kids too, and we live in the Rockies!

We've learned not to give in. Instead of telling kids exactly what to do or letting them stay inside, encourage them to explore and find something to do on their own. They may sit on the ground for a while and pick at the grass, but eventually their boredom will turn to curiosity. They will figure it out. Their natural instinct will take over.

Lean In to Kids' Curiosity, Creativity, and Imagination

If your kid sits on the other end of the spectrum, where they are already tapped into their curiosity and imagination and creativity, then double down on that. If you know the beach or a woodland is their thing, then plan more outings. Sign them up for camps. Encourage them to keep journals or bring home cool rocks.

If your kid loves to draw and do art, bring paints and crayons and markers outside and have them create what they're seeing. Get a journal and take them to a nature center or park, or even a yard will do too, and have them draw maps with landmarks. Ask them questions like, "What do you think caused that pipe to be above ground?" or "What do you think happened to that tree?"

Get them to tell you a story about what they're seeing outside.

By leaning in to their curiosities and interests, we reinforce to our kids that what they like matters, it's meaningful, and it's okay for them to have these interests. If our kids see that we're excited and supportive, they will embrace their interests more because they feel accepted.

As Reena B. Patel said, "We talk so much about following your passion, but the way I look at it, let's not follow our passions. Let's follow our curiosity, because if we follow that, we're always questioning: What is something? What are we going to do? And we're going to try and figure it out, and that becomes motivating."[23]

You may not actually be interested in or excited about what your kid likes. Kids and parents can—and do—have different interests. But this isn't about us. It's about the kids. It's about us loving them so much as the unique little people that they are and wanting them to be happy. It's about showing your sincere excitement for the curiosity they have by nurturing their interests.

LIFE LESSONS

If we're looking, nature has powerful metaphors for life. We can pass these onto our children to help them understand this world and their place in it.

It was nature that ultimately helped one of Taylor Ross's patients, a seven-year-old girl, understand what death was and that her beloved grandmother was dying of cancer. Taylor, a trauma-informed parenting and education consultant, was teaching the young girl's mother how to talk with her daughter in a way that she could understand death and what that meant. Taylor suggested the mother take her daughter into the woods and talk to her about logs, what they are, what they used to be, and how they help the forest grow, stay healthy, and continue the life cycle.

So the mother wandered through the forest with her daughter and they found a log. Sitting next to it, they watched the bugs crawling on moss. They talked about what moss was and how the log had once been a part of a tall, beautiful tree.

As the little girl looked and touched the log, her mother talked to her about life and death and what was happening to her grandmother, using the tree and log as a metaphor. As Taylor recalled, "The little girl got it right away. She said to her mother, 'Oh, Grandma's not going anywhere; she's becoming something else like this log that lives on through other bugs that eat the wood.'"[24]

By removing ourselves from nature, we have removed the natural lessons about life, death, and cycles, as well as the unexpected, unplanned, and uncontrolled and resiliency.

But it's still there buried in our DNA. We come from nature, and to nature we shall return one day. Helping our kids connect to nature now, and also showing them the lessons that it has to teach them, will awaken what has been forgotten but not lost forever.

Richard Louv said he was surprised by how much support he received from religious leaders of all faiths after he published his best-selling book, *Last Child in the Woods: Saving Our Children from Nature-Deficit Disorder.* "From conservative fundamentalists to Hindu to Christian to Jewish to indigenous leaders, I was surprised, but maybe I shouldn't have been, because I've come to the conclusion that smart religious or spiritual people understand that all spiritual life, whatever kind, originates in a sense of wonder. When is it that we first feel wonder? What window or doorway do we go through into wonder? I think for many of us, it was like my experience."[25]

Richard said he remembered being a young boy and crawling to where the grass ended and the rocks and trees began. He vividly recalled, at the age of three, turning over a rock and realizing he was not alone in the universe. "There was life under that rock and listening to the sound in the trees . . . it sounded like a voice to me, and I felt connected to something far larger than myself, larger than my parents, larger than what I was already beginning to see on television, and it filled me with a sense of wonder and awe."[26]

Getting our kids outside and connecting with nature helps to develop that sense that there is something bigger that animates the natural world—whatever you want to call it. It takes kids out of the anxieties and stresses and pressures and prefabricated fantasy worlds and places them squarely back in their bodies, tapping into their spiritual sides.

Using nature will also give them a place to turn to when they're feeling down or sad, or even lonely. In a recent study, 40 percent of young people between the ages of 16 and 24 reported feeling "often" to "very often" lonely.[27] This was the highest reported level of any age group and reflects that there is something happening to the coming of age right now unique to their generation.

But nature heals. The more time our kids spend outside connecting to their natural environments, the less lonely they may feel.

Conscious Parenting Suggestion: Introduce Stillness

Our kids—and we too—love the rough-and-tumble activities that leave us huffing and sweating. There is absolutely a place for that. And we try to offset those moments with stillness, reverence, and deep gratitude and appreciation for the natural kingdom.

You can do the same with your kids by taking them to the beach, the edge of a cliff, sitting beneath a tree, or watching the sun rise or set. If you can, try to find a time when there aren't as many people around and you can sit and be with them. Let them stare out. No talking.

Just be in the moment; let your minds and hearts return to stillness.

Within these moments, we will feel something much more powerful and bigger than ourselves. It requires nothing from us or our children. It's a gift from the universe.

You can instill in your kids, right now, this deep connection and appreciation for nature and ability and wisdom to know that when they face struggle and uncertainty and fear, they may turn to nature for answers, solace, and wisdom. It may take a few tries to get your kids to sit still—or even for you to sit still. We aren't used to just being present, but it's so good for us. Try not to get too frustrated if it takes a few passes for everyone to get comfortable.

Stick with it because if you can teach this to your kids, you have given them a priceless treasure.

BECOMING CONSCIOUS

It was a Saturday morning, and the family had just finished breakfast when Micah and Noah started fighting. They were bickering and shoving each other, and something inside of Jim snapped. "That's enough!" he shouted. "Stop it right now. Go to your rooms. Change your clothes. We are going to the beach."

The boys looked stunned. The beach was almost a two-hour drive away. When the family went, which was only a handful of times a year, it was always planned well in advance. When the boys didn't move, Jim looked at them, smiled, and said, "I'm serious. Go get your stuff. I'm leaving in 30 minutes. Anyone not in the car gets left behind."

It was like the gates of heaven opened. The boys' demeanors changed, and they raced to get ready. Going to the beach was one of their favorite places. It was an unexpected day trip, but Jim, Lesley, and the boys had a blast. The kids spent the day in the water and in the sand—even better, they didn't fight at all.

That night, after the boys had fallen asleep—early—Jim told Lesley that he wanted to start planning an outing every weekend. Whether it was to the beach or to hiking trails or up to the park, he wanted to find more ways to get the boys outside. Lesley said she was onboard but wondered if he'd have time.

"I think I have to make time," he told her. Lesley said she was game too. She had never hiked before and didn't consider herself an outdoorswoman, but she would try it all with her boys, and if there were some things that Jim wanted to take the boys on solo, she'd understand.

Lesley's enthusiasm gave Jim an extra dose of inspiration. He spent his nights researching and finding hiking trails and nature parks within a two-hour drive. Surprisingly, there were more than he thought. At first, the boys weren't sure what to expect and didn't seem keen on spending time hiking or in the woods, but once he got them there, they took to it almost immediately. Lesley too.

One time when they were hiking, the boys wanted to go off trail. It made Lesley nervous, but Jim said they could go for a bit. Jim let the boys lead the way, as he assured Lesley that he knew how to get them back to the main trail. The family made their way down a little embankment and discovered a small river. There were stumps and rocks, and Jim and Lesley found a spot to sit while the boys turned over stones and shouted to one another about the cool-looking pebbles they found. They wanted to try building a dam, and Jim and Lesley watched—almost stunned—at how the brothers were cooperating and working together to find sticks and stones. The dam didn't work, but Micah and Noah had fun being immersed in the building of it and being outdoors together.

It was an extraordinary experience, and that night, Lesley told Jim that if she had any doubt about this "nature thing," she had become a true believer.

Their weekend outings became an amazing family-bonding experience. It was something everyone looked forward to, and eventually the boys became involved with planning and picking where the family was going. Admittedly, not every weekend worked out. But even when they had short windows, Jim and Lesley made it a point to take the boys to the nearest park.

It didn't take long for Micah's behavior to improve either. His outbursts became less frequent and not as supercharged. He also didn't seem to fight as much with his brother, which made the entire household more peaceful. Jim and Lesley are still working on finding ways to get Micah and Noah outside more regularly than the once-a-week outing. While that remains a challenge, they believe it's something they can overcome eventually, especially because they've included Micah in the conversation, asking him how and what he would like to do.

Conscious Parenting Challenge

Mark your calendars! For one month, we challenge you to schedule a weekly nature session. Put it in the schedule and honor it like you would a doctor's appointment. What you do is up to you. We would encourage you to get outdoors with your kiddo, but if that's not possible, then at least get them outdoors alone. For an extra challenge, schedule twice-weekly sessions, and if you want to stretch this, make it a daily event. Have fun with it. Encourage your kids to have fun. Nature is fun and healing, so just get them out there and let them explore and see for themselves.

CHAPTER 9

STEALING TIME

Dan and Annie believed in exposing their three children, Katelin (15), Josh (13), and Trevor (10) to *everything*.

Some of this was out of guilt. When the kids were very young, Dan and Annie divorced, and while they were committed to co-parenting productively and knew that they were not meant to be married, they worried that the kids were "missing out" somehow. Giving their kids opportunities to get involved in anything was a way to "make amends." Dan and Annie wanted to raise kids to become productive and successful members of society, which to them meant being well rounded and involved in numerous activities.

So when the kids' school system took away foreign language classes due to budget cuts, the parents hired a tutor. (Annie had read that learning a second language was critical for brain development.)

Then the kids needed piano and guitar lessons.

And sports—soccer, basketball, softball, and baseball.

And drama and community service clubs.

Neither Dan nor Annie ever stopped to wonder if the kids' schedules were too much. Sure, the kids were incredibly busy and it felt like a full-time job coordinating rides and figuring out who would go to what game. But Dan and Annie had both happily remarried, so they were lucky to have extra drivers, and the kids had an extended family to support, love, and help them manage.

Plus, Dan and Annie prescribed to the conventional "always-be-hustling" culture. The two worked full-time, running their own businesses, and they truly believed that the more they and their kids did, the more likely they were to succeed.

The kids had never complained. They just went with the flow and seemed content leading full lives. It wasn't until Trevor started having epic meltdowns over the smallest of things—losing a board game, knocking over a glass of juice, being late to a practice—that Dan and Annie started worrying that something was off with all their children.

That's when they started to notice the bags under their kids' eyes, how hard it was to get them up in the morning, the short, clipped responses to questions, and the near-panicked tones before tests or games.

It took only one session with a parenting coach for Dan and Annie to realize that they weren't raising three well-rounded, productive members of society—they were raising three balls of anxiety and stress who didn't know how to slow down and rest.

MODERN CHALLENGES

Time.

It's the most valuable resource we have. Once used, we don't get it back, and there is nothing we can do to make more of it. Given its worth, you'd think that our society would have learned how to use it more wisely. Instead, many parents are squandering huge sums of cash and their energy reserves by keeping their kids busy—in most cases, too busy.

Whether it's school, sports, or clubs, our kids are spending their precious childhood time living on never-ending merry-go-rounds of doing that leaves them exhausted, overscheduled and overworked, and riddled with anxiety and fear. The pressure to keep going is enormous, but we're too busy ourselves to notice what's happening. And even if we can see, most parents don't know what to do about it, because *it's life* and everyone is living like this.

That's not good enough. Our kids are developing dysfunctional relationships with their most precious resource, and if we don't turn this around now, we're setting kids up for regret and stress down the road.

We want to be very clear: we believe it's healthy for our kids to engage in extracurriculars.

Organized activities can help kids discover who they are, ignite their passions, and learn important life lessons. But kids need balance and to slow down. It is when they're resting and playing and relaxing that they learn to tap into their inner selves, repair and heal their minds and bodies, and restore their energy reserves.

Mastering time is about learning when to do and when to be. We can teach them how to do this, but that means letting go of our beliefs, expectations, and societal pressures to stay busy.

We aim to help you do that for your kids, yourself, and your family.

We know the immense pressure you probably feel to expose your kids to every opportunity possible. Keeping them busy is often a choice made from love. Wanting to give your kids what you had or didn't have and wanting them to find their place in the world, their interests, and where they can shine brightest drive many of our decisions.

But we encourage you to reevaluate how your child spends their time—because they won't get any of this back. Neither will you. Let's teach them how to spend their most precious resource wisely and intentionally.

LIVING LIFE OVERSCHEDULED

While all of us can rationalize and justify the reasons why our kids lead such busy lives or turn to their devices when they have a free minute, there are very real costs that our kids pay from this punishing lifestyle.

Namely, they miss out on valuable free time where they can be kids and play.

Play? Do we even know what that word means? It's so easy for parents to forget this, let alone have playtime and downtime themselves. Our society runs off being overworked. What parent isn't? And this is true whether parents carry a job outside of the home or not.

We have been conditioned by our culture to feel pride over working late into the night and filling our schedules. Downtime isn't seen as a luxury, let alone a necessity—it's a sign of laziness. Or potentially worse, "I'm not a good enough parent if my kid doesn't . . ." or "If I don't give my child every access and opportunity to do . . . then I've failed as a parent." Even conscious parents fall into the overscheduling trap without recognizing the dark side.

All animals—and yes, that includes us—have two settings: doing and being.

By overscheduling our kids, we keep their minds and bodies in constant stimulation and under intense pressure. A constant state of doing keeps their nervous systems jacked up on the hormones adrenaline and cortisol, which can lead to anxiety, GI issues, headaches, and other health-related conditions. The more our kids keep going and going, the greater risk they have for burning out and becoming exhausted.

Kids need time to unwind and relax. When they shift from doing to being, their minds and bodies are able to heal and repair themselves as their nervous systems move from the high-energy, fight-or-flight mode into rest and digest. When kids slow down, their creativity, imagination, and problem-solving abilities rise to the surface.

We understand, it's not easy to slow down, limit activities, and make space for kids to be kids. Teaching your kid how to just *be* isn't always accepted. You may feel pressured by extended family, friends, or your own judgments and beliefs that tell you to keep your kids constantly involved in extracurricular activities, sports, and extra classes or tutoring.

But keeping our kids on the merry-go-round now will only make it harder for them to get off later. They won't know how to relax, play, or have downtime as adults because they will have never learned it. They will be more susceptible to burnout, stress, and anxiety. The state of being will feel foreign to them and wrong—although it's one of the healthiest, most self-nurturing practices they will be able to give themselves that will also make them better people, partners, workers, and possibly parents.

Parents need this too. Everyone is spinning so fast that we're one spin away from breaking. We can get out of this cycle. It's doable. But it takes admitting that we have a problem first.

Doing this will not make you a "bad parent." It will not condemn your kids to a lifetime of mediocrity. You may be surprised how dialing back on the doing and increasing the being actually catapult your kid ahead in education, health, and happiness. They deserve this opportunity, and so do you.

Conscious Parenting Suggestion: Give Kids More Free, Unstructured Playtime

We can choose to practice the art of being by taking control of time, rearranging commitments, saying no more often, and saying yes to more play and free time.

Schedule Free Time

Kids need downtime to play and not in front of a device. They need unstructured free time where they're outside or making up games or playing pretend. This is their soul food. This is when they get to find their interests and likes.

It takes us intentionally giving them that time and space. That may mean scheduling it and making it a priority. If you're looking at your kids' calendars and you can't find *any* openings, then that could be a sign it's time to reconsider what they're involved in.

Are they playing multiple sports and engaged in extracurriculars? Are they spending too much time on homework and tutoring or extra classes? Are they passionate about everything they're involved in, or can they drop something?

It's highly effective to have these conversations with your children. Some of the answers may be age dependent. When kids hit middle to high school years, it's easy to get involved in a lot of activities. Your child may even insist everything is important. It takes a willingness to be very candid and to closely examine the benefits and costs.

It might be that you decide that it's important for them to have 30 minutes of free time before they go to bed without devices or screens. Or it could be that there's a block of time every weekend that's reserved for free time.

Getting free time into their calendars can—and will—look different for each kid and family. But just like we want to get our kids eating healthy foods, we need to get them having more downtime too. Talk with your kids about why it is a priority. And then find a solution. It can be done.

Give Yourself Downtime

Downtime? As a parent? *Impossible,* you probably say. *Those two things can't go together.* Or can they? We believe that if we have any hope of teaching our kids how to slow down and avoid the overscheduling lifestyle, then we have to find ways to live that truth for ourselves.

We're not saying that's easy, just that it's necessary.

Sometimes parents aren't overscheduling their kids, but kids still feel pressured and anxious. It may come from expectations that we're nonverbally communicating to them. If we're constantly working late into the night and early morning, if we're always on our devices, if our kids never see us chilling, laughing, or having a good time, then that sends a message. It tells kids that relaxing and slowing down is bad and there's something wrong with that.

The more we can model taking care of ourselves by finding a healthier balance in our schedules, the easier it will be for our kids to embrace that lesson too. When they see us relax and keep a doable schedule, it says to our kids that it's acceptable and okay.

We're willing to bet that you probably need this just as much—maybe more—than your kids. Not that we need to give this to you, but in case you need to hear, you deserve to slow down and say no to getting involved and filling your calendar with every request.

And in case this wasn't clear enough before, it is okay for our kids to be bored. Boredom inspires creativity, imagination, and curiosity. By dialing back the activities, slowing down, and giving time back to our kids, they reap so much more—physically, mentally, and emotionally.

WHAT'S BEHIND ALL THAT DOING?

Susie Walton, a parenting educator and teacher, remembers how her son Luke was six years old when he told her that he was going to play in the NBA like his dad, Bill Walton. She believed him. "Ask any of his brothers—I have four sons—and they will say they knew from the beginning that he had it in him," Susie recalled.[1] "This guy had the strongest desire to play ball. It was always in him, and I never once had to say, 'If you want to make the NBA, you better go shoot fifty free throws,' or 'I'm going to hire you a trainer so you're in the best shape.' He just had the internal drive, and as a result, he played ten years in the NBA."[2]

If you stepped back from your kids' activities, would you still see a passion and drive for them? We sure hope so. Because that internal drive turns into *inner motivation*—the jet fuel that will propel your kids forward in life. It will get your kids much further in life than external motivations such as the need to make tons of money, buy the biggest house, and have the fanciest job title.

Too often, it's the parents who insist their kids get involved in activities—not because the kids are passionate about them, but because the parents are. "It's common that we transfer what we didn't get or didn't do as a child onto our children," said Reena B. Patel, a child and educational psychologist.[3] "Oftentimes, I see children in activities that they have no interest in, but when I talk to their parents, I learn it was the parents who really wanted to be a part of that T-ball team or quarterback of the football team, and it was really their dream when they were kids."[4]

As Reena explained, we need to pause and see our kids clearly while asking ourselves the brutally honest questions like: What is it that *they* want? What is it that *they* are interested in?

This calls back to some of our key conscious parenting philosophies. We have to be willing to heal any old wounds and to see our kids as they are—not as we wish or want or expect them to be. The more we can embrace these philosophies, the easier it'll be for you, your kids, and your family.

And we want to assure you that if your kid falls into the camp where they're doing things where you're the driving force, that does not make you a bad parent. At some point, we've all enrolled our kids in activities or pushed them to explore avenues that they didn't want, weren't interested in, or maybe were scared of. Kids often don't know what they like until they try something, but they're not always the most open and receptive to new experiences.

Cut yourself some slack. You want the best for your kids, and you're motivated to give them every opportunity that you can give them.

Commit to doing it differently going forward. However your kids spend their time today, it can be changed for tomorrow.

Conscious Parenting Suggestion: See Clearly

Once we see our kids clearly—their likes, passions, interests—the easier it will be to find the right activities and ways for them to spend their time.

Be Honest about Your Motivation

This is the tough talk portion of our programming where we ask you to take an honest look at the reasons why your kid is involved in whatever activities fill their days. This means we have to embrace self-awareness and recognize if we're pushing our kids to do things because we loved them or wish we had had the chance to try them.

If you have to drag your kid to their activities, then perhaps they are involved in the wrong ones. Ask yourself, *Do they light up when they're doing the activities? Do they have to be poked and prodded to keep going?*

Has your kid tried the activity long enough to know if they're the right ones? We mention this because sometimes kids will try an activity at an early age, and it may not initially work out simply due to the newness of it.

Sometimes we have to weigh the value of giving our kids time to grow and improve to the point where they can enjoy it versus recognizing it's just not their thing and letting it go so they can try other activities.

There is no universal right; it's what's right for your kid. If you make that concept your guiding star, then your kids will not get lost. You will, in fact, show them the path to who they are.

Give Kids Time to Discover Themselves

Sometimes it dawns on us that we don't know what our kids are into. If that's you, don't despair. Reena suggests that we allow kids to explore. It takes time for them to learn about the world. You may have a budding artist who excels at working with clay, but they have to experience it first.

Be patient. There's no rush. Our kids will discover their interests and passions and likes in their own time. But we can, and should, encourage it. We can expose them to different activities. We can pay attention to the kinds of play and toys they like. We can notice the kinds of shows or stories they're drawn toward. These can all be small clues that help us to help our kids find their fit.

COMPETITION: THE GOOD, BAD, AND UGLY

We can't talk about time compression and the volume of activities that pack our kids' days without mentioning competition. It's a cornerstone of what—and why—our kids get so involved with extracurriculars.

Hyper-competition drives much of the childhood experience today.

Competition can be healthy for kids, preparing them for life after childhood. "Our kid will have losses in real life," explained Reena B. Patel, a child and educational psychologist.[5] "They may not get the job they want. It may go to someone who our kids think they're better than. We need to prepare kids for this, and they need to learn what it's like to fail."[6]

Whether it's a science fair, a sports team, or a part in the school play, our kids may not reach the upper echelons, and it's healthy for them to face disappointment, loss, and sadness. Healthy competition can help them strengthen their inner resiliency so that as they grow into adulthood, they can face the inevitable challenges that everyone faces head on.

This is true for winning too. Putting in the hours to develop and master a skill teaches dedication, focus, and motivation. Setting a goal, working to achieve it, and attaining it (or striving to do so) are invaluable lessons for kids to learn that will pay dividends as they get older, not to mention all the other incredible traits like respect for their opponents, good sportsmanship, and celebrating and feeling proud of a win without gloating and making other kids feel bad.

Competition in this sense is hugely beneficial for kids. But a strong foundation of self-worth needs to be established first. As Alyson Schafer, an Adlerian family counselor and one of Canada's leading parenting experts and therapists, explained, competition becomes problematic when our kids learn to tie their performances, how they look, and outcomes of an event to their sense of self-worth and value as a person.

"Children who are raised to be competitive worry about how they look compared to others," explains Alyson.[7] "They have this mistaken idea that somehow their worth is elevated when they have certain outcomes like winning the Little League game, getting an A on a test, winning the science fair, or whatever it might be. And that's not true. The truth is, if they get an A in math, they know more about and have mastery of a skill. That doesn't make them a better human being."[8]

What we're seeing today is an epidemic with kids who have become fixated on competing with their peers to validate their worth and value as a person.

At the same time, the world that gets projected to them through entertainment, television, and social media tells them that if they want to live a "good life," then they must be as wildly successful as possible. That means possessions, wealth, money, power, prestige. To get those things, kids have to compete. In this mindset, being one's best is about being better than everyone else, where winning means they're better.

These parallel messages are damaging our kids and will leave them ill-equipped to navigate the choppy waters of life. Moreover, it is damaging to our collective society and communities.

Think about how often you get praised and recognized. It's probably not very often.

With most of the hard things that adults have to do in life, we do not receive accolades for them. Our sense of self-worth and value as a human being cannot come from the external world that is uncontrollable, unpredictable, and fleeting.

We can teach our kids, right now, that their value comes from within. That no one person is superior to anyone else. We're all inherently equal. We are all worthy of love, dignity, and respect.

We can show our kids that they are good and worthy—that they were born this way and they will always be this whether they win the chess competition or swim meet or land that prime spot on the competitive dance team.

If we can help them build self-esteem that's disconnected from winning and losing, then competition becomes an opportunity for them to challenge themselves, to see what their capabilities are, to grow and develop, and to experience failure and how to move through it.

This is how they will win at the game of life—by winning the inside game.

Conscious Parenting Suggestion: Teach Kids What Really Matters

When it comes to competition, we want our kids to feel internal motivation and have a solid self-worth foundation. We have a chance to teach our kids to connect to their being and know their value as a human being—not a human doing—and in the process, create real meaning in their lives.

Teach Kids to Turn Inward
In Dr. Carl Totton's clinical psychology practice, many patients arrive feeling unfulfilled, unsatisfied, and unhappy. They have spent their lives doggedly pursuing and obtaining all the material, external rewards that they can—and that they were conditioned to. They have followed the path that society told them would bring

them success, but somewhere along the way, how they felt about themselves and their authenticity got lost.

Dr. Totton has to go all the way back to their childhood to unwind the lessons they've learned about competition, success, and fulfillment. He has to take the focus from the external, material world and shine the lens on their internal worlds and true being.

He does this by asking them five questions that they—and all his patients—must answer if they're going to have a meaningful life:[9]

- **Who am I?** Everyone has to answer this question sooner or later. If the answers provided come from external sources of validation, then the person usually does not know who they are.

- **Where am I coming from?** This is about knowing their personal history, the traditions passed down in their family of origin, and their culture. It's their connection to their past, ancestors, and stream of time.

- **What are my values?** What has been embedded in someone from the community or family that they grew up in? What have they absorbed and what do they believe in with every fiber of their being? Values are what they stand for and are nonnegotiable, such as truth, compassion, fairness, and respect.

- **What do I love?** What are they passionate about? What do they love to do with their time? What lights them up? What interests them that they would choose to do if they had the means?

- **What is my special gift that I have to offer the world, and what should I be doing right now?** This question has to be answered as adults, because it guides people toward what they should do and what is most meaningful for them in the future.

"The shamans who I've studied with, they say that shamans dream their lives into existence," said Dr. Totton.[10] "In the vast universe, there are unlimited potential realities and possibilities that are out there somewhere. Since they are out there as authentic possibilities, they've already happened to some extent. It's through our individual searching for answers to these five questions that we can dream our futures into existence."[11]

Dr. Totton says that through the course of our parenting, if we can help our children learn to ask and answer these questions, we will teach them how to find fulfillment, satisfaction, and contentment *within* themselves as adults.

"If a parent and family unit can nurture these attributes and provide their children with an internalized sense of values that motivate them to dream their realities into existence, kids will have a very high achievement level, because they now source their power from their own sense of authenticity," explained Dr. Totton.[12]

Bringing this into practice starts with letting go of the comparison games and excessive external validation. Comparing one child to another, or siblings even, can lead to a deep sense of poor self-esteem and lack of confidence, Dr. Totton explained. It will also keep kids focused on having to win, be the best, and continually reaching for external sources of fulfillment, satisfaction, and contentment that prove their worth and value.

This is a process; it's not a one-and-done game to play with our kids. We can take the questions that Dr. Totton listed and start to seed them into our kids' consciousness. We can ask our kids to think about these questions, even if they don't have the answers. We can help our kids by seeing them for who they are and identifying their internal traits, unique skills, and family traditions, and talking with them about it.

Think slow and steady—and repeat.

It also helps if we ask ourselves the same questions. If we don't know the answers, then that's an answer too. The more we know ourselves and find our power from within, the better we can guide our children. Tell your kids about what you value, where you came from, your unique gifts, and what you're doing with them in this world.

"The main task of a parent, besides protection and providing for a child's financial needs and a place to sleep, is providing a sense of containment and nurturance, so that they can discover who they are and feel supported as they move forward in becoming who they are," said Dr. Totton. "If a parent can do that, they've done a good job."[13]

Redefine Success

Attaining wealth, power, and possessions—that's the definition of "success" kids grow up with. Kids believe if they check the boxes on these items, happiness and meaning will be theirs.

Except it's a myth.

Dr. Carl Totton practices near Hollywood. Many of his clients are highly successful in the business, entertainment, and music industries. Yet even when they are the image of success, something can still be missing. "They can, literally, have hundreds of millions of dollars sitting in the bank, and be the most miserable people you've ever met in your life," explained Dr. Totton.[14]

"Growing up, they got fed the bill of goods that if they just acquire and get more and more successful in terms of material possessions, then that was the key to a happy life. Now they've done it and realized it wasn't true. Financial success has very little to do with how content and happy we are with ourselves and in our lives."[15]

What if we started to redefine success for our kids today? What if we taught them that success and leading meaningful, fulfilled lives is about being true to themselves? That it's about tapping into their passions and interests, talents and gifts, and using them in ways that contribute to the world in a positive way?

It is okay for them to want nice things, to have a great job and financial security, to have prized possessions, and to develop skills that let them (potentially) rise to the top of their chosen field.

But these external outcomes do not define success alone.

Instead it's knowing and loving who they are—strengths and weaknesses, failures and triumphs—and appreciating, respecting, and finding joy in the experiences that make up their lives.

If we can give our kids this wisdom, we will set them up for a lifetime of meaning and fulfillment.

BECOMING CONSCIOUS

Dan and Annie's parenting coach explained that their kids needed more downtime to just be kids—to play, hang out, and chill. The parenting coach suggested that Dan and Annie do one thing with their kids: decompress.

This meant they needed to pare back the kids' schedules. Per the parenting coach's advice, Dan and Annie called a family meeting to talk about how this would work. They wanted each child to be fully engaged in picking and choosing what activities to keep and what to drop.

During the family meeting, Dan and Annie were honest and open, sharing their thoughts and feelings and apologizing for unintentionally placing unrealistic expectations on their kids to stay busy and do all of these activities.

Going forward, Dan and Annie explained that there were going to be some limits placed on activities. First, one sport per season. Each kid played three sports and participated on travel teams. The travel teams would stop so the kids could focus on the in-season sport.

Second, each child could only participate in two activities at any one time.

Third, Sundays were going to be for resting, relaxing, and spending time with family. Whether the kids were at their mom's or dad's didn't matter. There would be no scheduled events, but "family time."

Their oldest, Katelin, pushed back. She wanted to know if she could still hang out with friends. Naturally, this created a chain reaction with Josh saying that if his sister could hang out with her friends, then he wanted to hang out with his friends too. But Dan and Annie held firm, saying that they would try a Sunday Family Time routine for one month and then they'd reevaluate. Everyone agreed they could do this for a month.

As the family meeting came to a close, Dan and Annie were surprised by how little their kids fought the changes. And in the week ahead, the kids seemed to like them. Each kid picked the two activities that they really wanted to do and dropped the ones they didn't. That alone seemed to restore the kids' energy.

Overall, the changes went smoothly, although some didn't happen as quickly as Dan and Annie had wanted. For instance, since it was the middle of spring, Katelin was playing softball for her high school team while also playing on a travel basketball squad. She felt that if she dropped basketball immediately, she'd leave her team in a lurch and her friends would "hate" her. She also enjoyed playing basketball. Many of her tournaments were on Sundays too, which interfered with the family time rule the parents had put in place.

Instead of telling Katelin what she had to do, Dan and Annie asked her what she wanted. It was Katelin's idea to make an upcoming tournament in five weeks her last one. It was the biggest tournament, and she felt that she could tell her coach and teammates that after that, she would be stepping back to focus on her other commitments. Katelin felt that would be fair to everyone.

Dan and Annie agreed and told Katelin how proud of her they were for coming up with this solution. (And they really were!) The only request they made of Katelin was that after she played in the final tournament, Katelin give the Sunday Family Time a real shot—and she agreed.

Dan and Annie had no idea how powerful these seemingly small adjustments to the kids' calendars would turn out to be. At different times, each kid told Dan and Annie that they loved coming home because everyone—especially their parents—seemed less stressed out. People laughed and joked around more, and people hung around more instead of there being a constant stream of doors closing, grabbing and eating food on the go, and passing interactions.

Life seemed lighter, and family time actually became a thing that even Katelin enjoyed. (She never told them, but she also never asked to hang out with her friends instead.)

Dan and Annie never meant to burden their kids with too many to-dos. They honestly believed they were giving their kids opportunities and a leg up in the world. And their kids, like most kids, just went with the flow because being busy was all they knew.

But they learned it's never too late to step back and reevaluate how their kids spend their time and adjust accordingly. It meant paying attention and taking the lead, talking to their kids, dialing back, and working together to find what works best for them.

Conscious Parenting Challenge

It's break time! We challenge you to review your kids' schedules and revaluate every commitment, from extracurriculars to school to sports to socializing. Then we encourage you to find something to let go. You can combine this with the previous challenge to give your kids more unstructured time outside. It may be hard at first—doing and always being on the go can become addicting—but within a couple of weeks, your kids will likely relax into the space, feeling lighter, happier, and less stressed. Bonus challenge: give yourself some break time too.

CONCLUSION

We have so little control over our children, yet so much power to influence who they become.

We've shared dozens of suggestions, stories, and hopefully, deepened your awareness about what you and your kids face today. No matter what suggestions we give you—or any book or expert for that matter—when it comes to parenting and raising kids, the best lessons come from *you*.

Our children learn so much from us. Educational psychologist Dr. Michele Borba shared a powerful story with us that we want to leave you with. She told us about one of the best pieces of research she had ever seen that helped her understand empathy and raising kids. It came from a social psychologist who interviewed rescuers during World War II. The psychologist wanted to understand why some people became altruists, so they interviewed hundreds of rescuers.

Everyone said the same thing: "It was how I was raised."

The researchers discovered that the rescuers shared three common experiences from their childhoods.

They had watched their parents. The rescuers were raised by parents who were the epitome of kindness and modeled what they wanted their children to absorb. Whether that was to be respectful, responsible, kind—whatever traits the parents modeled, their kids absorbed.

Their parents had expected them to behave. Rescuers were raised with clear right versus wrong behaviors. They grew up knowing that their parents expected them to display certain traits like kindness and respect. If the rescuers had misbehaved, say they were disrespectful or cruel, then there were consequences.

Their parents had given them opportunities to do good. The parents would say, "Let's go bake cookies for the neighbor next door," or "Grandpa looks sad. What can we do to help him feel better?" It was through ongoing opportunities that kids realized they were caring, kind, respectful people.

"Kids act how they see themselves to be," said Dr. Borba.[1] "What we have to do is plant in them how we want them to see themselves, and then tune up our behavior, because we are the images that our kids will catch."[2]

It was Dr. Borba's last comment that gutted us: "We are the images that our kids catch." It is the essence of this book. She isn't talking about what jobs our kids will have when they're adults, what colleges they attend, the kind of home they may live in, or any of the material possessions that our modern world pushes on us.

Dr. Borba was talking about who our kids become on the inside. What qualities and values will they inherit and learn to embody because of us? What kind of person do you want to teach them to be? Look in the mirror, because that's who they're learning to be.

Conscious parenting is absolutely about our kids, but we—parents—are at the heart of this movement. At the end of the day, raising kids is about who we are—how we show up, how we respond, what we say, and what images we model that our kids will catch.

Every experience we shared with you comes back to one thing: your awareness and the actions you pair with it. Awareness without action doesn't work. Action without awareness doesn't work either.

Will you get this right all the time? No way! It's okay to mess up. In fact, it will happen. Nobody is perfect. Your parents weren't, nor were your grandparents or great-grandparents. Frankly, it's a rite of passage for all kids that Mom and Dad get some stuff wrong.

It's okay to make mistakes. How else do we reach consciousness if we don't first recognize when we're acting unconsciously? Do your best. Start by setting the intention to be conscious—to be fully present in the moment—with your kids. When you do that, change begins *inside* of you. Then the world opens. When you show up differently, your kids will respond and react differently.

And we can't leave the conscious parenting world without also mentioning that this is not just about you or your child; it's about the collective consciousness of the world too. We are raising kids in a time of unprecedented strife and struggle, but there is hope and possibility too. It lies with our children and the vision for the world that they will create and dream into existence. They can learn to be unconscious or conscious. They can learn to live distracted or present. They can learn to extend compassion, respect, and kindness or project judgment, disrespect, and cruelty.

You cannot control who your child ultimately becomes or what they do as adults. But you can greatly influence them. You can give them a foundation that allows them to walk into adulthood with confidence, assertiveness, connection to themselves, emotional and spiritual resiliency, and mental fortitude.

All of this is born and inspired from their relationship and bond with you. Show up. Be present. Tune in. See and hear and accept them for who they are. Love them. Enjoy your time with them. Have fun together.

Teach, guide, and help your children grow.

ENDNOTES

Chapter 1

1. Greg Steckler, interview with the authors, May 16, 2019.
2. Laura Kalmes, interview with the authors, February 5, 2020.
3. Ibid.
4. Dr. Stephen Cowan, interview with the authors, February 12, 2020.
5. Ibid.
6. Taylor Ross, interview with the authors, November 12, 2019.
7. Jenny Carr, interview with the authors, December 9, 2019.
8. Ibid.

Chapter 2

1. Robin Ray Green, interview with the authors, November 13, 2019.
2. Dr. Christian Gonzalez, interview with the authors, February 19, 2020.
3. Haley Kaijala, interview with the authors, March 11, 2020.
4. Ibid.
5. Margaret Nichols, interview with the authors, February 12, 2020.
6. Ibid.
7. Haley Kaijala, interview.
8. Ibid.
9. Margaret Nichols, interview.
10. Ibid.
11. Laura Kalmes, interview.
12. Ibid.
13. Ibid.
14. Katie Kimball, interview with the authors, August 8, 2019.
15. Ibid.

16. Dr. Sam Rader, interview with the authors, September 12, 2019.

17. Ibid.

18. Ibid.

19. Ibid.

20. Ibid.

21. Ibid.

22. Ibid.

23. Ibid.

24. Laura Kalmes, interview.

25. Dr. Julie Brown Yau, interview with the authors, September 12, 2019.

26. Ibid.

Chapter 3

1. "Screen Time and Children," American Academy of Child and Adolescent Psychiatry, accessed October 2020, https://www.aacap.org/AACAP/Families_and_Youth/Facts_for_Families/FFF-Guide/Children-And-Watching-TV-054.aspx#:~:text=Screen%20Time%20and%20Children&text=Children%20and%20adolescents%20spend%20a,spend%20up%20to%209%20hours.

2. Common Sense Media, "New Report Finds Teens Feel Addicted to Their Phones, Causing Tension at Home," May 3, 2016, https://www.commonsensemedia.org/about-us/news/press-releases/new-report-finds-teens-feel-addicted-to-their-phones-causing-tension-at.

3. Dr. Elisa Song, interview with the authors, August 11, 2019.

4. Ibid.

5. Richard Louv, interview with the authors, March 12, 2020.

6. Ibid.

7. Ibid.

8. Reena B. Patel, interview with the authors, February 5, 2020.

9. Alyson Schafer, interview with the authors, February 12, 2020.

10. Ibid.

11. Katie Kimball, interview.

12. Ibid.

13. Trina Wyatt, interview with the authors, August 21, 2019.

14. Teodora Pavkovic, interview with the authors, June 13, 2019.

15. Ibid.

16. Ibid.

17. "Board Games Market—Global Outlook and Forecast," Reportlinker, December 11, 2018, https://www.prnewswire.com/news-releases/board-games-market---global-outlook-and-forecast-2018-2023-300763553.html.

18. Ibid.

19. Ibid.

20. Ibid.

21. Michael Robb, "Common Sense Media Census Measures Plugged-In Parents," Common Sense Media, December 5, 2016, https://www.commonsensemedia.org/blog/common-sense-media-census-measures-plugged-in-parents.

22. Teodora Pavkovic, interview.

23. Ibid.

24. Ibid.

Chapter 4

1. Haley Kaijala, interview.

2. Ibid.

3. Dr. Stephen Cowan, interview.

4. Ibid.

5. Ibid.

6. Dr. Michele Borba, interview with the authors, February 12, 2020.

7. Susie Walton, interview with the authors, March 12, 2020.

8. Ibid.

9. Haley Kaijala, interview.

10. Hank Lutz, interview with the authors, September 12, 2019.

11. Ibid.

12. Dr. Stephen Cowan, interview.

13. Taylor Ross, interview.

14. Ibid.

15. Sarah Nannen, interview with the authors, November 12, 2019.

16. Ibid.

17. Ibid.

18. Andrew Marr, interview with the authors, October 29, 2019.

19. Ibid.

20. Dr. Michele Borba, interview.

21. Ibid.

22. Ibid.

23. Ibid.

Chapter 5

1. Gus Lubin, "There's a Staggering Conspiracy Behind the Rise of Consumer Culture," *Business Insider*, February 23, 2013, https://www.businessinsider.com/birth-of-consumer-culture-2013-2.

2. Ibid.

3. Ibid.

4. Gabi Jubran, interview with the authors, November 13, 2019.

5. Ibid.

6. Stacey Robbins, interview with the authors, August 8, 2019.

7. Laura Kalmes, interview.

8. Ibid.

9. Dr. Michele Borba, interview.

10. Haley Kaijala, interview.

11. Ibid.

12. Laura Kalmes, interview.

13. Ibid.

14. Haley Kaijala, interview.

15. Ibid.

16. Ibid.

17. Ibid.

18. Laura Kalmes, interview.

Chapter 6

1. Gabi Jubran, interview.

2. Heather Miller, interview with the authors, October 3, 2019.

3. Ibid.

4. Susie Walton, interview.

5. Ibid.

6. Ibid.

7. Laura Kalmes, interview.

8. Ibid.

9. Laura Kalmes, interview.

10. Ibid.

11. Robin Ray Green, interview.

12. Ibid.

13. Ibid.

14. Heather Miller, interview.

15. Ibid.

16. Ibid.

17. Laura Kalmes, interview.

18. Ibid.

19. Reena B. Patel, interview.

20. Heather Miller, interview.

21. Ibid.

22. Dr. Michele Borba, interview.

23. Ibid.

24. Stacey Robbins, interview.

25. Ibid.

26. Ibid.

27. Ibid.

28. Dr. Michele Borba, interview.

29. Ibid.

30. Ibid.

31. Heather Miller, interview.

32. Dr. Michele Borba, interview.

33. Ibid.

34. Ibid.

35. Ibid.

36. Ibid.

37. Ibid.

38. Ibid.

Chapter 7

1. Jenny Carr, interview.

2. Jenny Carr, interview.

3. Ibid.

4. Ibid.

5. Katie Kimball, interview.

6. National Institute of Environmental Health, U.S. Health and Human Services, "Flame Retardants," July 2016, https://www.niehs.nih.gov/health/materials/flame_retardants_508.pdf.

7. United States Environmental Protection Agency, "The Inside Story: A Guide to Indoor Air Quality," accessed October 2020, https://www.epa.gov/indoor-air-quality-iaq/inside-story-guide-indoor-air-quality#tab-2.

8. Ibid.

9. Trina Felber, interview with the authors, August 9, 2019.

10. Julie Matthews, interview with the authors, August 8, 2019.

11. Ibid.

12. Dr. Christian Gonzalez, interview.

13. Trina Felber, interview.

14. Centers for Disease Control and Prevention, "Data and Statistics on Autism Spectrum Disorder," accessed February 2021, https://www.cdc.gov/ncbddd/autism/data.html.

15. Ibid.

16. Centers for Disease Control and Prevention, "A Snapshot of Autism Spectrum Disorder in New Jersey," accessed February 2021, https://www.cdc.gov/ncbddd/autism/addm-community-report/new-jersey.html.

17. Dr. Darin Ingels, interview with the authors, August 8, 2019.

18. Ibid.

19. Ibid.

20. Ibid.

21. Ibid.

22. Ibid.

23. Ibid.

24. Ibid.

25. Ibid.

26. Ibid.

27. Adams, et al., "Comprehensive Nutritional and Dietary Intervention for Autism Spectrum Disorder—A Randomized, Controlled 12-Month Trial," *Nutrients* 10(3), 369 (March 2018), https://doi.org/10.3390/nu10030369.

28. Ibid.

29. Julie Matthews, interview.

Chapter 8

1. Kate Snow and Cynthia McFadden, "Generation at Risk: America's Youngest Facing Mental Health Crisis," *NBC News*, December 11, 2017, https://www.nbcnews.com/health/kids-health/generation-risk-america-s-youngest-facing-mental-health-crisis-n827836.

2. Ibid.

3. Richard Louv, interview.

4. Ibid.

5. Ibid.

6. Ibid.

7. Ibid.

8. Park Rx America, "Park Rx America: One Doctor's Perspective on Prescribing Parks," accessed November 2020, https://parkrxamerica.org/dr-robert-zarr.php.

9. Ibid.

10. White, et al., "Spending at Least 120 Minutes a Week in Nature Is Associated with Good Health and Wellbeing," *Scientific Reports* 9, (June 13, 2019), https://doi.org/10.1038/s41598-019-44097-3.

11. Ibid.

12. Richard Louv, interview.

13. Summer Lall, interview with the authors, February 5, 2020.

14. Ibid.

15. Dr. Ana-Maria Temple, interview with the authors, August 10, 2019.

16. Tiana Mondaca, interview with the authors, October 29, 2019.

17. Ibid.

18. Robin Ray Green, interview.

19. Ibid.

20. Reena B. Patel, interview.

21. Ibid.

22. Richard Louv, interview.

23. Reena B. Patel, interview.

24. Taylor Ross, interview.

25. Richard Louv, interview.

26. Ibid.

27. Claudia Hammond, "The Surprising Truth About Loneliness," *BBC*, September 30, 2018, https://www.bbc.com/future/article/20180928-the-surprising-truth-about-loneliness.

Chapter 9

1. Susie Walton, interview.
2. Ibid.
3. Reena B. Patel, interview.
4. Ibid.
5. Reena B. Patel, interview.
6. Ibid.
7. Alyson Schafer, interview.
8. Ibid.
9. Dr. Carl Totton, interview with the authors, September 11, 2019.
10. Ibid.
11. Ibid.
12. Ibid.
13. Ibid.
14. Ibid.
15. Ibid.

Conclusion

1. Dr. Michele Borba, interview.
2. Ibid.

INDEX

education, 91–109
bullying and, 100–107
curiosity and, 100
homeschooling example, 91–92, 107–109
homeschooling pros and cons, 98–100
modern-day challenges of, 92–93
nature for life lessons, 145–148
parental involvement in, 93–94
preparation for future with, 97
pressure of testing and grade, 94–97
recognizing strengths in children, 97, 109
emotion
addressing fear, 60–61
developing empathy, 49, 105–106
emotional intelligence, 48–51
fear and media/technology consumption, 43–48
food-body connection, 119–120
parents' calm confidence for, 59–61
postpartum depression, 24–27
toddlers' independence and dependence, 30–34, 36
See also existential threats
empathy, developing, 49, 105–106
empowered action, 68–69
EPA (Environmental Protection Agency) Product Standards, 124
exercises. *See* Conscious Parenting Challenges
Exhausted (Polizzi and Shojai), xiii
existential threats, 57–73
"comfort of us" as remedy for, 67–71
communication about, 64–67
example, 57, 71–72
modeling calm confidence for, 59–62
modern-day education environment and, 92–93
overcoming fear of outdoor play, 143
overexposure to graphic images and, 62–63
reframing, 58–59
teaching self-care for, 61, 67, 73
eye contact, 49–52, 54

F

failure. *See* mistakes
fear from existential threats. *See* existential threats
Felber, Trina, 123, 124
fight-or-flight mode, 44

flame retardants, 122
food-body connection, 119–120
food storage, 122, 124
fragrance-free products, 125
free time. *See* time issues
furniture, toxins in, 122, 124

G

game night, 49–50
gender issues
body image, 82–83
gendered toys, 86–87
genes, conscious conception and, 19
gluten-free foods, 115
Gonzalez, Christian, 20, 123–124
"good breast" experience, 28–29
Good Enough Infancy (Rader), 30
grades, 94–97
Green, Robin Ray, 19, 98–99, 143
green furniture, 124
growth buttons, 6

H

habits, changing, 6–7, 120
See also toxins
HAPPI (Helping Awesome Parents Parent Intentionally), 78, 84
healing. *See* self-care
health and nutrition
boosting health with nature (*See* nature)
creating healthy diet, 117–120, 129, 132
nutrients in recipes, 121
of parents-to-be, 19–20
during pregnancy, 20–24
toxin exposure in diet, 113–117 (*See also* toxins)
two-week challenge to eliminate processed sugar, 132
HEPA filters, 124
homeschooling
example of, 91–92, 107–109
pros and cons of, 98–100
See also education
hydrogenated oils, 116, 118

I

independence of toddlers, 30–34
See also early childhood development

ACKNOWLEDGMENTS

We are indebted to our wives and our children, who support and put up with us when we decide to write another book.

Our sincerest thanks to our contributors who gifted us with their wisdom and insights on conscious parenting, including Taylor Ross, Hank Lutz, Reena B. Patel, Sheila Kilbane, Katie Kimball, Dr. Sally LaMont, Gabi Jubran, Jenny Carr, Christian Gonzalez, Robin Ray Green, Heather Miller, Sue DeCaro, Trina Felber, Katie Wells, Julie Matthews, Anthony Youn, Ana-Maria Temple, Pejman Katiraei, Roseann Capanna-Hodge, Carl Totton, Sam Rader, Julie Yau, Greg Steckler, Opher Brayer, Teodora Pavkovic, Rebecca Phillips, Stacey Robbins, Tara Hunkin, Terry Wahls, Darin Ingels, Elisa Song, Jessica Sherman, Trina Wyatt, Andrew Marr, Tiana Mondaca, Sarah Nannen, Gabrielle Kaufmann, Laura Kalmes, Summer Lall, Linda Goldsmith, Alyson Schafer, Isa Herrera, Margaret Nichols, Michele Borba, Stephen Cowan, William Hufschmidt, Haley Kaijala, Richard Louv, and Susie Walton.

To our film and production crew, who dedicated hours to taping and interviewing our contributors. Lorenzo Phan, Mileen Patel, Courtney Donnelly, Sean Rivas, Carl Lindahl, and Dave Girtsman, this book wouldn't be possible without your commitment to excellence and extraordinary teamwork.

To Amanda Ibey, your uncanny ability to take reams of raw material, extract the most valuable insights, and weave it all together into prose leaves us humbled and grateful. You always make our projects better than we expect. To Courtney Donnelly, thank you for being our stalwart reader, providing notes on early drafts, and supporting us through this process.

Finally, we owe a huge debt of gratitude to Reid Tracy and Patty Gift at Hay House. Thank you for believing in us and our projects. It's been an honor and privilege to have you in our corner. And to our editor, Lisa Cheng. You made this book stronger with your insightful notes and passion.

ABOUT THE AUTHORS

Dr. Pedram Shojai is a man with many titles. He is the founder of Well.Org; the *New York Times* best-selling author of *The Urban Monk, Rise and Shine, The Art of Stopping Time, Inner Alchemy,* and *Focus*; and the co-author of *Exhausted* and *Trauma*. He is the producer and director of the movies *Vitality, Origins,* and *Prosperity*. He has also produced several documentary series, including *Interconnected, Gateway to Health,* and *Exhausted*. In his spare time, he's a Taoist abbot, a doctor of Oriental medicine, a kung fu world traveler, a fierce global green warrior, an avid backpacker, a devout alchemist, a qigong master, and an old-school Jedi bio-hacker working to preserve our natural world and wake us up to our full potential. You can find him online at www.theurbanmonk.com.

Nick Polizzi is a producer and director of feature-length documentaries about holistic alternatives to conventional medicine. He is the founder of the Sacred Science, director of the feature documentary by the same name, and author of the book based on the film. He is also the co-author of *Exhausted* and *Trauma*. Nick's mission as host and executive producer of the docuseries *Remedy: Ancient Medicines for Modern Illness* is to honor, preserve, and share powerful, evidence-based healing technologies with those who have been failed by modern medicine and the system as a whole. He has been traveling the world, documenting forgotten healing methods, ever since he cured himself of a debilitating illness at age 25 using a traditional therapy. You can visit him online at www.thesacredscience.com.

Hay House Titles of Related Interest

YOU CAN HEAL YOUR LIFE, the movie, starring Louise Hay & Friends
(available as a 1-DVD program, an expanded 2-DVD set,
and an online streaming video)
Learn more at www.hayhouse.com/louise-movie

THE SHIFT, the movie,
starring Dr. Wayne W. Dyer
(available as a 1-DVD program, an expanded 2-DVD set,
and an online streaming video)
Learn more at www.hayhouse.com/the-shift-movie

THE TAPPING SOLUTION FOR PARENTS, CHILDREN & TEENAGERS: How to Let Go of Excessive Stress, Anxiety, and Worry, and Raise Happy, Healthy, Resilient Families, by Nick Ortner

TURN AUTISM AROUND: An Action Guide for Parents of Young Children with Early Signs of Autism, by Mary Lynch Barbera, Ph.D. RN, BCBA-D

WILD THING: Embracing Childhood Traits in Adulthood for a Happier, More Carefree Life, by Mike Fairclough

All of the above are available at your local bookstore,
or may be ordered by contacting Hay House (see next page).

We hope you enjoyed this Hay House book. If you'd like to receive our online catalog featuring additional information on Hay House books and products, or if you'd like to find out more about the Hay Foundation, please contact:

Hay House, Inc., P.O. Box 5100, Carlsbad, CA 92018-5100
(760) 431-7695 or (800) 654-5126
(760) 431-6948 (fax) or (800) 650-5115 (fax)
www.hayhouse.com® • www.hayfoundation.org

———

Published in Australia by: Hay House Australia Pty. Ltd.,
18/36 Ralph St., Alexandria NSW 2015
Phone: 612-9669-4299 • *Fax:* 612-9669-4144
www.hayhouse.com.au

Published in the United Kingdom by: Hay House UK, Ltd.,
The Sixth Floor, Watson House, 54 Baker Street, London W1U 7BU
Phone: +44 (0)20 3927 7290 • *Fax:* +44 (0)20 3927 7291
www.hayhouse.co.uk

Published in India by: Hay House Publishers India,
Muskaan Complex, Plot No. 3, B-2, Vasant Kunj, New Delhi 110 070
Phone: 91-11-4176-1620 • *Fax:* 91-11-4176-1630
www.hayhouse.co.in

———

Access New Knowledge.
Anytime. Anywhere.

Learn and evolve at your own pace
with the world's leading experts.